Away...

FOR GOD'S SAKE

With Best Wishes

Kathleen Byrne

PRAISE FOR *AWAY... FOR GOD'S SAKE*

"It has been an honour and a pleasure reading your memoir. What a life you have lived! I have been captivated, moved to tears and moved to laugh out loud too.

It is a great read and what a treasure for your clan!"

— *Sorcha O'Malley, editor*

"A captivating life story that tugs at the heartstrings and highly entertains.

I'm familiar with the term 'Flying Nuns' but the 'flying corset' story is one of the funniest tales I've ever read!"

— *Award-winning author Wendy Scott*

Away...
FOR GOD'S SAKE

Kathleen Byrne

Published 2021
by Kathleen Byrne

ISBN 978-0-473-59240-0 (Softcover)
ISBN 978-0-473-59242-4 (Epub)
ISBN 978-0-473-59243-1 (Kindle)

Printed by Anglo Printers ltd
Mell Industrial Estate, Drogheda Co. Louth, Ireland. www.angloprinters.ie

Front cover photograph: Martin McNamara

For my wonderful parents Richard and Catherine Byrne,
my siblings, daughters and grandchildren.

Part 1

What lies behind us and what lies before us are
tiny matters compared to what lies within us
– Ralph Waldo Emerson

Chapter 1

WHERE IT ALL BEGAN

"Isla, Put the kettle on; Kitty has another girl."

Basie Wherity, a kind neighbour, shouted from upstairs to Aunt Isla, my father's sister, below. Isla lived with her mother in Dublin, 20 miles away, and had come to Balbriggan to look after my father Dick and my mother Kitty's four other children.

Isla's ear was glued to the old crackling Pye radio on that Thursday afternoon, it being her only enjoyment. Because of her short-sightedness, reading a book or going to the cinema was out of the question. Newspapers were a rare commodity at the time. So was practically everything else at the beginning of the third year of World War II. On that particular day, rain and a strong wind rattled the windows and doors of the terraced house in Drogheda Street. Bad weather continued throughout the bitterly cold northern winter of 1942. Pearl Harbour had been attacked a month earlier in December 1941, so shipping in and out of Ireland was at a standstill, which meant there was no coal being imported from Britain. Foodstuffs were pitifully scarce, and money scarcer still.

Isla filled the kettle. She had done so many times, flitting continually between the water pump in the street to the range and back again to the radio. Hoping that the top of the range would keep hot enough to make tea, and having gone to the empty coal-hole under the stairs to find some pieces of firewood that she pushed into the range, she reached for the tea caddy kept on the high mantlepiece overhead. A deep sigh escaped her lips as she scraped out the remaining few tea leaves.

My father, Richard (Dick), had gone to his workshop in Church Street to sweep up sawdust and wood shavings, which he tied in a piece of sackcloth like a Christmas pudding. He whistled a lively tune knowing its contents would keep the range going for heating and cooking, especially if he dampened it down a little. On his way home, he parked his bicycle at McMahon's grocery shop on the Square, where the depleted stock was supplemented with eggs and vegetables from "out the back". His shopping list was short; flour, an ounce of loose tea, and if his luck was in, maybe a couple of Sweet Afton. Goods were sometimes exchanged for nails, screws, wire or a piece of glass, all of which Mr McMahon would use to maintain his chicken run and pigsty. Nearly everything was rationed. My father was well known for his cabinet making and carpentry skills. He had contacts where he could forage out some black-market soap, candles, margarine, and even a few ounces of sugar. He then called at McCann's grocery shop and public house on the corner of Bridge Street and Mill Street, where he regularly did repairs to floorboards, windows and doors for Annie McCann.

Arriving home on this January evening, as he started to climb the stairs to welcome the new arrival, he came across my brother. Nine-year-old Nicholas was seated on the bottom step, his head held in his hands. Looking up sorrowfully at his father, he asked in a mournful tone, "Daddy, why did the nurse bring another girl in that black bag?"

Nurse Cooney carried a black leather bag when entering patients' homes. Children, therefore, thought this was how babies were delivered.

"Well, son, we have to take what God sends us."

"But I have three sisters already."

The poor boy was inconsolable at not having a brother like all his friends in the street. Most of the neighbouring large families had boys. My parent's eldest daughter, Monica, was just ten months younger than Nicholas. Helen was nearly six years old, and May would be three years old in three months' time.

Dressed in the same silk and lace christening robes used for my older siblings, I was baptised 'Catherine Frances Byrne' two days later, on Saturday 31st January 1942. My godmother, Aunt Isla, held me in her arms as George Dickson, who owned the garage and petrol pumps in Drogheda Street, drove us to St Peter and Paul's Church, Balbriggan. My father's apprentice Patrick Sullivan, my godfather, wore his first pair of long trousers for the occasion.

Car ownership was confined to professional people. Petrol was rationed, scarce and used only if absolutely necessary. People walked for miles everywhere if they didn't have a bicycle or a pony and trap. Even the milk was delivered each morning by Jackie Campbell in his horse and cart, while Peggy Denis jumped off the cart to fetch the three-quart cans left outside on window sills. Old tin buckets containing ashes that had been raked from the range and left out weekly were emptied into "The Gub" Corcoran's wooden, horse-drawn cart. All other rubbish was burned to provide heat. Water had to be drawn from a pump in the street. Sanitary arrangements consisted of a small, white-washed dry toilet at the bottom of the garden. This provided for the whole family, and the neighbours' toilet was adjacent. Private conversations took place in this loo or behind the hen shed. The local postman at the time asked Dick to make a double seat for his outside toilet so that two of his many children could use it at the same time and thus avoid a queue.

Life continued to be harsh for the Byrne family throughout the remaining war years. But it was less harsh than for other families who suffered unemployment and hardship. Being self-employed, my father managed to get jobs making new furniture, as well as repairing, restoring, and renovating antiques. My mother had acquired great personal and economic skills while employed by a lady named Mrs Stoker in Leeson Park, Dublin. As the sole employee in the household from the age of 14-years-old, she had performed the duties of housekeeper, lady's maid, cook, cleaner, and scullery maid "below stairs".

It was while she was in this employment that she met my father. When she left home in Clarkstown in County Louth, my grandmother had told her to visit her Aunt Maggie in Dublin on her days off. These were limited to one free day per month. Maggie was my grandmother's sister, and she was married to John Gibbons. John's brother Pat was also married to a girl called Maggie. Both families lived on Dublin's northside. Pat's wife had a nephew named Richard Byrne, who often came to visit and hang around with his cousins. On one particular sunny afternoon when all the cousins were meeting before going for a swim at the North Wall, Richard was introduced to Kitty. They were in no way related to each other, but each of them had cousins who in turn were related through marriage. Kitty was shy and hardly looked at the young man. Richard was born on 15th May 1907 to Nicholas and Ellen Byrne and lived at 7 North Court Avenue in north Dublin. The family consisted of four boys and four girls. I never knew either of my grandfathers as they were already deceased before my birth.

Richard was very handsome and was not backward in coming forward in his romantic pursuit. After many persistent invitations to Kitty to go for a jaunt in the sidecar attached to his motorbike, she capitalised on the offer. She said she would like him to take her to see her older sister Lizzie who was working as a nanny with the Macken family in Naul. This was the start of a fine romance. He gave her a beautiful pearl necklace for her 21st birthday. A blue sapphire engagement ring came next, and they were married in Donnybrook Church in Dublin in September 1933.

At this time, Richard was employed by 'Joiner' Rooney in Balbriggan on the construction site of the Savoy Cinema. He had board and lodgings with the Misses Mary and Marcella Mangan at St Molaga's Terrace. When a house in Drogheda Street became available to rent from the Cumiskey family, Richard and Kitty began married life in No 2 Peacock Villas and lived there for the remainder of their lives. Terraced, the house was wedged between No 1 and No 3, with spiked black railings dividing the three very small gardens from the footpath.

In 1933, Balbriggan was a small, close-knit industrial town on the east coast of Ireland. Having been attacked by a regiment of British soldiers called the Black and Tans thirteen years earlier, the local Deeds, Templar & Co. factory, public houses and many houses were torched and completely burned. These acts were in reprisal for the fatal shooting of a member of the Royal Irish Constabulary. Locals were employed either in Gallen's Mill, Smyth & Co. or Deeds, Templar & Co. hosiery factories, in agriculture or fishing industries.

My parents had come from very different backgrounds. My mother was born and baptised in Stamullen, County Meath, of a generation of people who worked hard on the land. If they could be described in one word, it would be decent. But there was also an element of finesse about them. My maternal grandmother often spoke of being visited by her great aunt, who would arrive regularly at their humble abode in a horse-drawn carriage that only the aristocracy could afford. Lady Jane Ffrench, her great aunt, who had remained a spinster, regularly brought gifts of clothes and food in secret to the impoverished members of her sister Catherine's family. Such generous visits were kept secret because her sister Catherine had been disowned and disinherited for having fallen in love with and subsequently marrying Tommy O'Brien, the village blacksmith's apprentice. This scandalous act had been deemed unworthy of her station in life. Ever since, there has always been a girl named Catherine in every generation of the family, right down to the present day.

My father, on the other hand, had been born and reared on the northside of Dublin city, of modest parents who originated from Feltrim and St Dulough parish. In a city where, at the time, there existed a tremendous class divide, my father's family could be described as respectable. Religion was high on the agenda. Hard work was a strong ethos, with each member of the family made aware that the devil made work for idle hands. Abstinence from alcohol was strictly observed and was still adhered to by my father throughout his lifetime. From a young age, he was apprenticed to a cabinet maker, where he learned his trade. He became a connoisseur of fine furniture and antiques, could recognise each type of timber, fretwork, inlay and joinery at a glance, and was a skilled upholsterer.

Nothing was wasted in our house. Pots of dumpling stew bubbled on the range. Apple tarts, brown soda bread, blackberry pies and custard were cooked in the range oven. A chicken run provided eggs and chicken soup. Barney Kenny's cockerel was a frequent visitor to the hen shed, and chicks were hatched on a regular basis. Rabbits were bought from Jazzy Garvey, who arrived at our door every Saturday, with dozens of dead rabbits tied to the crossbar of his bicycle. My mother often haggled with him for the price of the rabbit from half a crown down to two shillings. The rabbit, skinned and washed, would then be stewed with vegetables. We ate fish on Fridays as this was a day of abstinence from meat, with a fry up on Saturday mornings of sausages, black and white pudding, with eggs and rashers of bacon. In an era when the word recycling was unheard of, it came naturally to us. Worn-out flannel sheets became nappies, dusters and dishcloths. Crumpled old newspapers were dampened and used for window cleaning; shirt collars were taken off and turned; old overcoat seams were ripped, resized to fit a younger member of the family and stitched on my mother's Singer sewing machine. Chicken bones and marrow bones were boiled until the water drained and cooled, forming a jelly that was used to cure ills and chills. Wool from worn-out woollen hand-knitted garments was retrieved and rerolled into balls to be knitted again. Glass jars became vases to hold wild dog daisies, primroses, and bluebells.

Petrol and gas were in short supply. Rationing had been introduced by Eamon de Valera, the then Taoiseach of Ireland, in 1941. The rationing of foodstuffs meant that we lived frugally but on a very healthy diet of root vegetables, eggs and fish. My brother Nicky went to the empty coal yard at the harbour with a bucket and shovel to sweep up any coal dust that might be still there. This could be used in the range with wood and paper. He brought home fish from the harbour, which had been thrown up onto the quay by Jemmer Richardson. Hanked with a nail through the gills and threaded onto twine, this bounty would provide us with a hearty meal. Some items could be obtained on the black market from Northern Ireland, which was and still is part of the United Kingdom. On one occasion, my father got wind of the word that a consignment of loose tea was to arrive at J.F.'s grocery shop. He parked his bike outside, and a queue formed behind him. J.F. had just opened the large tea chest.

"The rogues, the rogues!" J.F. could be heard shouting.

He shouted more mild obscenities while people looked through the shop window. The poor man was on the verge of hysteria upon discovering that he had been hoodwinked. Instead of tea, the chest was filled with turf mould and stones.

Chapter 2

MALACHY WORE A COLLAR OF GOLD

My brother Richard Malachy was born on 10th February 1945, when I was three years old. Incredible as it may seem, I can remember it distinctly. Monica, Helen, May and I were gathered on our parent's bed upstairs, near the recess at the top window. We saw young Louis Kenny, who worked in Dickson's Garage, where there was a phone, running to our hall door letterbox, lifting the flap and shouting:

"It's a B.O.Y."

An excited discussion started amongst ourselves as to what the new baby would be called.

In those days, it was the custom to name children after their grandparents, uncles or aunts.

We'll call him Patrick after Uncle Paddy," suggested Monica.

"No," piped in Helen.

"We already have too many Paddies; Uncles Paddy Hoey and Paddy Byrne. He should be called Thomas, after Granda Hoey."

May said he should be called Bonnie as in *My Bonnie Lies Over the Ocean*. It was her musical side emerging.

Little me butted in as usual:

"Let's call him Kathleen, 'cos he's after me."

My three sisters laughed until the tears rolled down their faces.

When the little urchin arrived home, he was so small he wasn't expected to live. He was placed into a cardboard shoebox beside the range. Twelve-year-old Nicky sat gazing at his little brother while Basie fed milk to the tiny baby from a rubber topped dropper. He was called Malachy Richard after an ancient king who wore a collar of gold.

I hated him. I refused to look at him. I didn't want him getting all the attention. I wanted to be kissed, cuddled and be called Kittens like it was before he came along. He got a new pram. My father made it. Blue with a black leatherette hood, the handle and suspensions were retrieved from another pram. The wheels were smaller than those on the old Silver Cross model we had all been ushered around in. Strips of leather allowed the pram to bounce on its suspensions. It was a masterpiece. Halfway down inside the pram, there was a platform floor with a little trap door leading down further into the bottom half. This area was used to transport anything that could be gathered, bartered or foraged: crab apples, firewood, vegetables and blackberries.

Mammy and Basie would often wheel the pram across the beach to an area known as the flat banks by the Sailor's Grave, with us children trooping after them. Teapot, jam sandwiches and mugs were unloaded from the bottom of the pram. Stones positioned in a circle filled with crackling kindling held up the boiling teapot. Smoke never smelled so good. After a quick dip in the sea, we drank our sweet milky smoke-flavoured tea. All this was heaven to us. On one such occasion, while we gathered blackberries and kindling for the fire along the railway beside the sea, we heard Mammy and Basie shriek with delight at what they had found in the long grass at the embankment. Discovering big clumps of coal and calling it black gold, they quickly filled the bottom of the pram with this precious commodity that had not been available since before the war.

However, their joy turned to panic when they noticed the rising tide, which would cut them off from the homeward stretch. To add to this, the weight of the coal caused the leather strap holding the suspension to come adrift on one side of the pram. Monica carried baby Malachy in her arms while the two ladies pulled, hauled and dragged the lop-sided cargo over the shingle, rocks and wet sand that made up the narrow passage remaining between the high cliffs and incoming tide.

Help came in the form of the long arm of the law. Garda (PC) Boylan was having his daily swim. He spotted the group and came to their assistance. Wondering why the heavy listed vehicle was so difficult to drag, he tied it up with one of his garters. The women were terrified that he would see the coal. They knew it had been thrown from the Great Northern steam train on its way from Belfast to Dublin to be picked up by a contact and would have been considered stolen property. They also suspected the identity of the person who had missed out on a warm coal fire – someone whose relative worked stoking the steam engine.

Religion was a major influence in my childhood. My parents were devoted Roman Catholics. From an early age, we were taught prayer, obedience and respect. A great part of our daily lives revolved around faith and the liturgy. We attended Mass on Sundays and Holy Days of Obligation. Fridays were days of abstinence from all types of meat. The seven deadly sins, the Ten Commandments of God and the Six Commandments of the Church were constant reminders of Heaven and Hell. There was regular confession and communion. The Rosary was recited each evening in the living room-cum-kitchen. On our knees, facing the picture of the Sacred Heart, leaning on kitchen chairs, we recited the second half of the Hail Mary and the Our Father and then listened to my mother reciting the Litany of the Saints and the Virgin Mary.

Chapter 3

SCHOOLDAYS

I STARTED SCHOOL THE DAY after my 4th birthday, in St Peter and Paul's National School in Chapel Street, Balbriggan. Nicky and my three older sisters were already there; Nicky was in Mr Keely's class, May in Miss Reilly's, with Helen and Monica upstairs with Mrs Corcoran. It felt important to be with them. Mrs Connor, who had a room full of Babies, Infants and High Infants, put me sitting between Sean Campbell and Nuala Downes, who had been there from the previous September. They knew their ABC, the sign of the cross and could count to 10! Class started with the reciting of the Hail Mary and the Our Father prayers. I cried a little and often, but Mrs Connor was kind and gentle; we were her babies. She would tell us to fold our arms on the little individual tables and to put our heads down for a sleep. I was happy to have the use of a framed slate and chalk. After about two years with Mrs Connor, we progressed to Mrs Whitney's class. Things then became more serious. Tears, snotty noses or wet knickers were no longer tolerated. Wiping noses on the back of sleeves was forbidden. We were obliged to produce a hanky or a rag from our pocket or sleeve each morning.

The strict discipline was, however, compensated by the free lunches.

A stampede up the stairs led us to where Kitty White and her helpers sliced up thick wedges of Spicer's bread. Knives flashed as the women attempted to spread the butter. The result was that we either got a dry slice of bread or one with a great lump of butter on it. Cocoa was served in blue-rimmed, white enamel mugs if we were lucky enough to be there before they were all taken. There was never enough for everyone as mugs were nicked to be brought home.

Mrs Whitney prepared us for First Communion – a task she took very seriously. The priest would often visit to see if we were up to scratch on the Catechism. Shortly before my first confession, I was asked in class to perform a rehearsal of this ritual. Shaking with trepidation, I began:

"Bless me, Father, for I have sinned. Father, this is my first confession," I stuttered, thinking that was as far as I was supposed to go in front of the class.

"Continue," Mrs Whitney ordered several times, waving her stick.

I remained silent. Vera Delaney was then asked to recite her sins.

"Father, I stole a penny on Johnny Reynolds."

A gasp of shame followed as she sat down. Johnny Reynolds had a shop in Clonard Street. Vera had asked for a toffee bar, but instead of leaving her penny on the counter, she had run off with the toffee and the penny.

"Now, Cáit Ní Bhroin, let us hear yours," the teacher addressed me impatiently by my Irish name while waving her stick more vigorously.

I duly recited the example Vera had used. To my horror, the teacher waved her stick close to my nose, correcting my grammar.

"You stole from Johnny Reynolds too?"

"No, Miss," I stuttered, trying to explain.

"So now you are lying, and that's another sin you must confess and seek God's forgiveness," she roared.

I shook with fear at the injustice of her words but felt paralysed against arguing back. This incident inspired my fear of both God and teachers, which endured for a very long time.

My First Communion day was a memorable occasion for all the wrong reasons. It meant getting all dressed up in a white satin dress that had been specially made for me by Molly Andrews, a local young dressmaker who shared a workshop with Monnie Smith, above Tom Hagan's butcher shop in Bridge Street. My hair had been washed and twisted into pipe cleaners to make ringlets. A white lace-trimmed tulle veil was clipped with pins to my hair. A parcel posted to me a few days earlier by Aunt Isla, my godmother, contained a pair of black shiny patent shoes. The fact that I was the only first communicant approaching the altar wearing black shoes didn't bother me. My mother said they would last longer than the cheap white canvas shoes worn by everyone else. I was excited most of all about THE HANDBAG. Ah yes, this would, I hoped, be filled with sixpenny pieces, shillings and maybe the odd half-crown. My friend Mary Wherity also made her First Communion the same day. We went across the road to her grandfather Melia's house, where he lived with her granny and Aunt Mary. That visit yielded a few coppers, but when we went upstairs to where Mary's brother Jim slept, it was well worth our while. Jim opened his eyes and sat upright.

"Have I died and gone to heaven? I see two little angels," he hollered as he reached down to the end of the bed where his trousers lay.

He fished out a sixpence for each of us. Off we ran down the stairs, into the street and away to Shaw's sweet shop for goodies.

Chapter 4

PLAYING ALL DAY

IMMEDIATELY AFTER WWII, A FOREIGN family arrived in our town. Nobody knew anything about these people, except that they were called Dubrinsky. Keeping much to themselves, they lived in a beautiful thatched cottage on the outskirts of town. The single-story house was surrounded on three sides by a large garden, an orchard, and bordered by Kiely's farm at the rear. The properties were separated by a stream, a ditch and lots of trees. Kiely's barn was a popular rendezvous for us village youngsters. Old ropes and tyres hanging from the rafters were used as swings and trapezes, where Tarzans, monkeys and cowboy films were imitated and re-enacted. The steering wheel of an old, dilapidated Ford van less its wheels was fought over by all who wanted to be the driver. It remained stationary even when it became a fire engine, a bus or a police car.

On one fine day during the summer school holidays when it was too hot to stay in the barn, a group of us, ranging in age from four-year-old Malachy to 10-year-olds May and Jerry Kennedy, decided to explore the Dubrinsky domain. Crossing the stream, we crawled through the bottom of the hedges. Once inside, a magnificent sight enfolded before our greedy eager eyes. In addition to apple and pear trees, an abundance of raspberries, strawberries and gooseberries covered the entire garden. As we gazed in wonderous delight, Tom Kiely climbed the apple tree as a lookout saying that he would whistle if he saw anybody appear from the house. We attacked the fruit like locusts, gathering whatever we could in our pockets and our lifted skirts. A dog barked. Kiely jumped from his lookout post.

"Scamper," he yelled. "The auld wan has a gun!"

A shot rang out as we scrambled for our lives to the hedge and the stream, pushing and shoving each other. Some fell. Glancing back at May, I could see her holding her chest, where a big red stain appeared on her white blouse. She cried out loud in anguish, and someone shouted:

"May is after gettin' shot!"

Our screams and cries caused some neighbours and passers-by to gather round. As people assisted May to her feet, the red patch grew bigger.

"It's raspberry juice," she cried. "And I'll be murdered when I get home when Mammy sees my new white blouse."

We got a right telling off and were never allowed to frequent Kiely's barn again. May was severely reprimanded as she was supposed to look after the younger children and give good examples.

I was four years old when my little sister Frances was born. It was the summer of 1946. I had been taken to Drogheda with May to stay on holiday with Aunt Peg, Mammy's younger sister. Her husband, Tommy Kerr, worked in the old cement factory beside the River Boyne on the road leading to Baltray. Living at No 1 Bredin Street, they had three boys, Frankie, Tom and Desmond, and two girls, Mary and Margaret. Born at Our Lady of Lourdes Hospital in Drogheda, Frances was a beautiful baby. I remember getting my first glimpse of her as she arrived in Mammy's arms in Bredin Street. While seated on a small stool in the front room, my baby sister was placed in my arms.

May, Mary Kerr and I played all day making rag dolls and dolls' clothes. Sometimes we were joined by some of the other children living in Bredin Street. The Curran family lived on the opposite side of the street. As Mrs Curran was very generous with her jam and banana sandwiches, we were careful not to fight with or fall out with any of her many children. The Breen family also lived in Bredin Street. They were a large family of mainly boys. On rainy days we played in the little shed at the side of the house. We loved cutting up rags with scissors and sewing the dolls' clothes.

On Sundays, we were taken to the High Lane Church to attend Mass. The walk from Bredin Street seemed very long, and Mass appeared to last for hours. There usually was, however, a treat in store for us. Emerging out into the sunlight in Lawrence Street, much to our delight, Granny Mother, also attending Mass, was there with her pony and trap to greet us. Mounting the little iron step at the back of the trap and taking our places, we felt like aristocratic ladies. For us, it was today's equivalent of being chauffeur driven in a Rolls Royce. Up the Chord Road we cantered until Granny pulled on the reins outside a grocery and licenced premises. We remained in our seats while she tethered the pony to the electric pole. She went in and came out like a flash of lightning with her handbag under her arm. We never did find out what the purchased item was, but we suspected that the proprietor who knew her well had the message ready for her in a small bottle. A penny each was placed in the palm of our hands as we alighted from the trap back in Bredin Street. We quickly crossed the road to Sheila Matthews' little shop to spend our money.

It was during those summers spent in Drogheda that I heard the name of Oliver Cromwell mentioned for the first time. Scarlet Street took its name from the rivulets of blood that flowed there during the massacre at the siege of terror carried out by Cromwell and his army on 3rd to 11th September 1649 on behalf of British Parliamentary forces, against the Catholic Confederation and English Royalists. Not understanding history at the time, I shuddered hearing about the heads of innocents being paraded on pikes. The shrine of Saint Oliver Plunket in Saint Peter's Church in West Street contains the head of the martyred Irish Archbishop. It was usual for us children to be taken there to light candles and to pray for favours to be granted to us. I heard about these atrocities in early childhood, but I was never any good at history during my later schooldays. I could never remember the date of the battle of Clontarf, the death of Brian Boru, or the Battle of the Boyne. When asked a question during history lessons, my mind would just go blank no matter how much I had studied or reread the relevant chapter. This was perhaps because history consisted of invasions, wars, battles, cruel massacres and enmity between rival peoples. Subconsciously, stories of conquerors and invaders filled me with horror. Why would I want to remember what happened between greedy people hundreds of years ago? I realise now, however, that our history is important. It is why, how and who we are today. The oppression and struggle for freedom that the Irish nation endured for centuries is the reason for our identity and our independence. Our native Irish language has survived together with many facets of our Celtic cultural heritage.

Still believing that babies came in a black leather bag, when my little brother Thomas was born in March 1948, I was still in Mrs Connor's class. Arriving home from school on that day, I was distraught to find Mammy absent. Her coat was gone from the hook on the back door. A strange voice informed me that Mammy had gone to Drogheda and that I had another little brother. I looked up into the kindly face of Nancy Polis, who was to look after us. She made sure we were fed and washed. She scrubbed my knees so hard the scab that had formed after a fall bled and made me cry out loud.

I remember playing in the field at the back of our house in Drogheda Street. Long hours were spent outdoors in summer. As we had very few toys, we had to invent shops, post offices, ice cream parlours and schoolrooms. Role play was popular, but we didn't call it role play then. It was "pretend or make-believe". The shy child became a dominating teacher, and the meek suddenly became somebody important like a doctor, nurse or policeman. Pieces of broken china called chanies were used for money. Stones, shells, bits of coloured broken glass known as jelly stones and empty tin cans became objects of value. When we played house, elaborate plans were drawn out in mud, stones and pulled grass. Tea was water poured out into tiny cups and saucers. Bread and cheese were leaves gathered from the hawthorn bush. Old perfume bottles, empty tubes of lipstick and pieces of old broken jewellery retrieved from the ditch lined the shelves of our shop. Playing with Kay Brogan and Ann Smith was always exciting as their backyards contained lots of discarded household items. One day Ann produced a teapot and poured us a special drink from it. Fizzy and cold, we drank it quickly, not knowing that it was Andrews Liver Salts…resulting in the runs for the following few days.

My brother Nicky and my older three sisters seemed to be always busy. They appeared grown up and wise. I did not play with them as they were out and about with friends of their own age. If we went to the beach or blackberry picking, Monica and Helen would be in charge of looking after the younger members of the family. Next to each other in age, my sister May and I were very close. We were often sent on errands together. Obliged to take any of my younger siblings with us was deemed a nuisance. Malachy was small and slowed us down; Frances and Thomas, being wheeled in the pram, restricted our activities, especially if we wanted to run across fields or play hide-and-seek. The sight of these three beautiful blond curly-haired urchins elicited admiration from neighbours. People stopped to look at them. Because of my dark straight locks and scrawny appearance, I would stand back with a bowed head. During my childhood, I believed my parents were ancient. My father dressed in his working clothes most of the time – consisting of a pair of dungarees, a cloth cap and a tweed jacket. He wore a suit, necktie and trilby hat for Mass on Sundays. With this finery, he wore a white shirt with a starched detachable shirt collar fastened at the throat by a brass stud, with cufflinks holding his sleeves closed at the wrists. His sole source of entertainment was regular visits to the Commercial Club, situated above Kitty White's shop on the Square. At this all-male venue, members enjoyed a game of billiards, and lasting friendships were forged as town gossip and news were discussed.

My mother wore the same style of swagger coat for years. Preferring to wear a hat rather than follow the fashion of that era of sporting a square headscarf tied under the chin, she kept her hair, although it was grey, permed in short waves. Miss Mathews had a hairdressing salon opposite our house in Drogheda Street. When she made her way across the road to have her hair done, my mother would be gone for hours. It must have been a tremendous restful treat for her as each client would be seated in individual cubicles to be pampered in private. Ponds Vanishing cream went on her skin daily, and whenever she could afford to go to Dublin, she shopped in Clerys for a new hat and gloves. Her concession to luxury was a visit to the cinema. When herself and Basie went to see Bing Crosby and Ingrid Bergman in the black and white film The Bells of St. Mary's, they hummed and sang the soundtrack for ages afterwards.

There was always great excitement when the hay was being brought to the barn in Cumisky's farmyard. Dozens of children jumped on the low empty horse-drawn cart when it left the yard to collect the haystack. The driver, Mr Frank Hand, gave Miss Molly, the big brown mare, a lash of the whip or a pull on the reins as we headed off to the field down the Drogheda Road. When the cart was loaded with hay, only the lucky few could sit on the remaining space at the back. Those unfortunates who were left behind must run faster than Miss Molly in order to arrive in the yard and be first to jump on for the next trip.

Disputes and disagreements ended in hair being pulled and lots of pushing and shoving. When evening came, we were called home and back to reality.

The afternoon cinema matinée on Sunday was a great treat. In our family, it was customary after Sunday dinner to be given sixpence each for the pictures. There were two cinemas: The Savoy in Dublin St, and the old cinema on the Square. The Savoy was our favourite. It cost fourpence to get into the front section. With tuppence left, we hastened to spend it in Corcoran's o' the hill. Pauline Corcoran and her mother had a sweet shop on the corner of Georges Hill and Drogheda Street with shelves lined with large jars of sweets: bulls' eyes, Liquorice Allsorts, and our favourite Love Hearts. Toffee bars cost a penny and were lethal on teeth. Cleeves Toffee was sold by the square at two squares for a penny. Pauline was the first person in the town to make ice lollipops. They were red, raspberry flavoured, and made from the same cordial she served poured over the homemade ice cream in little bowls that could be enjoyed sitting at a table inside the shop. Balbriggan being a small town, everyone knew everyone else – who they were related to, what they did for a living and any other details of their lives, whether good or bad. Most people lived in rented housing, with newly married couples often moving in with their parents/in-laws. A row of thatched, mud-walled dwellings between Chapel St corner and Dickson's garage housed large families. Few of these houses had electricity. They were later replaced by the new Technical School in the early fifties. Graffiti was unheard of. The only vandalism that existed was a broken apple tree branch in Cannon Hickey's orchard, a ruined patch in the cornfield where lovers had lain, or a vacant spot in a turnip field where some hungry family members had helped themselves.

When we got to the cinema, Mr T.B. Connelly, standing at the door, made sure no miscreants slipped in without queuing up for a ticket. Mr 'Spider' Donnelly stood like a sentry man at the side entrance at the back near the stage. This door was used only as an exit when the pictures were over and, once opened, resulted in a stampede. Usherettes with flashing torches were on duty leading us to our seats and were on hand to keep law and order. If the film reel broke down, the audience erupted into mayhem and bedlam. When the film was about cowboys and Indians, everyone sat on the edge of their upturned seat, rising up and down in a galloping motion, thus obstructing the view of the person sitting behind. This caused rows with shouting and fisticuffs. We rode the ranges with Roy Rogers on his horse Trigger, Hopalong Cassidy, and Gabby Hayes, who we called Windy Breeches. There was always a serial running which kept attendance up, even in summer. Flash Gordon was the hero who inevitably won against the "bad lads".

When summer arrived, however, we took to the beach in droves. Learning to swim when I was six years old, I started doing the doggy paddle. My friend Niamh Kelly could swim a few strokes. I tried hard to compete with her. We then usually combed the beach area near the harbour wall for any buckets or spades that might have been left behind by the "Sunshiners". These were children from Dublin's inner city who were taken to Sunshine House in Balbriggan by the Society of St Vincent de Paul. A group of boys would stay for a week, and then a group of girls the following week. This pattern continued throughout the summer months. Gazing in awe into the playground attached to Sunshine House, at dozens of children our age enjoying the slides and swings, we often tried to sneak in unnoticed by the volunteer leaders guarding the gates. On one such occasion, we followed the queues of kids entering the building to get into the big refectory for the evening meal. As we hunkered down at a table, we were struck by fists and kicks from the ragamuffins whose places we had taken. Molly Johnston, the cook, appeared and quickly recognised us. We were quickly ejected off the premises and told not to come back. Jeff Sheridan was the caretaker and woe to any mischief-maker found on the property. Retreating, the noisy voices and laughter of the children inside could be heard from the road outside as we made our way home. Everyone competed to learn to swim on the front beach before progressing to swimming at the Black Rock, where there was a concrete bridge leading to the big rock. Concrete steps led down to ten feet of water at full tide. Queues of swimmers formed at the spring diving board, which was covered with cord matting – taking turns to run, dive or jump off. Being a very popular venue for old and young, people lounged there for hours, sunning themselves.

When I was about 13 or 14 years of age, the Red Cross started life-saving courses at the bathhouse beside the Martello tower. It is often said that on a fine day, the Isle of Man can be seen from the top of the tower. My friend Niamh and I signed up to do the course. We first did land drill, learning the skill of approaching the drowning victim without being pulled under ourselves. When the time came to practice in the water, it was very demanding but a lot of fun. While treading water, we had to take off our heavy clothes and shoes. We enjoyed it immensely and even passed our exams and gained certificates.

Chapter 5

NEARLY AWAY

MY FATHER'S BROTHER JERRY BYRNE and his wife, Lizzy, regularly came to visit us. Being childless, they greatly admired each of us. They lived in Dublin and travelled to Balbriggan by bus. Bringing sweets, cakes and biscuits, we were always delighted to see them. On one occasion, before leaving, they suggested that one of us could come and live with them. This was not an unusual occurrence in large families. Many children were taken to live with grannies or relations to relieve overcrowding, but also to help out on farms and to care for elderly kith and kin. When Lizzy and Jerry asked for volunteers, I shot up my hand. Perhaps it was because I knew that they had a beautiful house, had a huge aviary full of canaries and budgies in their backyard, or that I suspected, as their sole adoptee, I would be spoiled rotten.

I started to pack my paltry few belongings. Alas, it was not to be. It was not very often that my father interfered in the goings-on and the running of the household. This was considered the domain of my mother. But in this instance, he categorically and with great authority voiced his objection.

"She's staying where she is." And that was that.

Even though we lacked modern luxuries, we were happy. We were well fed, and there was always a warm fire in the range. When we were washed in warm, sudsy water in a big tin bath in front of the fire on Saturday, we emerged smelling of sunlight soap. Clothes were washed and scrubbed on a glass washboard in a tub on Mondays. Cleaning the house on Saturdays was a major chore shared by each member of the family. After the range was cleaned out, it had to be rubbed down with a substance called black lead; the steel edges were then sandpapered to remove spills of gravy or dribbles of porridge. Upstairs the beds were straightened out and corners of sheets and blankets folded in. The floors were swept and washed, and the patterned lino in the middle was polished. The black and red tiles in the hall were washed before the red tiles were individually polished with cardinal red polish. On the front door, the knocker and letterbox were shined with Brasso and elbow grease until glistening. In the front room, which was called the parlour, the mahogany table, surrounded by upholstered chairs, was dusted and polished. The top of the china cabinet filled with my parents' surviving wedding presents was adorned with The Child of Prague statue together with statues of Our lady of Lourdes and Fatima. The accompanying floral tributes were tidied up and replenished. All this cleaning and tidying was done without any modern convenience. The lack of storage space was never a problem because of the minimal amount of luxuries or gadgets we possessed.

My father loved auctions, especially auctions of antiques and household effects. He arrived home one day with one of the earliest Electrolux vacuum cleaners. My mother, viewing it critically, suggested that it would use up too much electricity. She knew that the arrival of a certain gentleman employed by the Electricity Supply Board was a constant threat to those who did not pay their supply bill on time. Mr

McGee could be seen regularly at front doors in the street, big clippers in hand ready to disconnect supply, leaving unfortunate families in darkness. My father's reply was that it would save her the time and trouble of taking the mats outside to be beaten. When plugged in for the first time, the said apparatus blew a fuse – leaving us in the dark for hours. On another occasion, my mother and Basie went to Sharkey's auction of household contents. My mother had mentioned to my father that there was a china basin and jug with a matching chamber pot in Sharkey's window that she fancied. Basie and herself arrived early and sat in the front row. Bidding for the basin, jug and chamber pot began at two shillings. My mother kept bidding up to ten shillings which was her limit. Two other bidders at the back continued until the said item went for twelve shillings and sixpence. When he arrived home, my father lamented that he had tried to buy the basin, jug and potty for my mother and that "some auld bitch up the front" had outbid him up to ten shillings. He had then let it go to the man beside him. He was never told who the wretch up the front was.

We played together, cried, fought together, and toasted bread or chestnuts pierced onto a long-handled toasting fork on the fire in the little fireplaces in the upstairs bedrooms in winter. We snuggled together under the Foxford blankets between the flannel sheets on the horsehair mattresses and pulled my father's heavy LDF (Local Defence Force) coat up over our heads. This heavy pale green hairy coat was part of the uniform issued to members of the LDF during the emergency between 1941 until the end of WWII. His unit belonged to "A" group. He trained in nearby Gormanston Army Camp. His boots seemed enormous. He would polish the brown leather spats and fasten them around his legs with pride. The sound of heavy marching could be heard from where we stood at our front door as we watched these soldiers, complete with their rifles, parade past. Although remaining neutral, Ireland was ready in the event of an invasion by Germany. Wedged between the United States and Britain, Ireland's Eamonn De Valera resisted joining the Allies, fearing a recurrence of the Civil War due to the remaining unease existing between Ireland and its nearest neighbour since Independence from Britain in 1922. The old coat remained and kept us warm long after the war ended.

Chapter 6

A SHATTERING BLOW TO HAPPINESS

THE SEASONS CAME AND WENT. Christmas was always wonderful. In the days leading up to the festivities, my mother pedalled furiously on her sewing machine, making new pleated tartan skirts for each of us girls. Daddy brought home a huge paper lantern in the shape of a star, which he hung around the light bulb in the hall. The whole family got up for First Mass at 6 am. Fasting, and trudging to the church in the dark, we could see the lighted candles in every window along the way. Santy always came, bringing us dolls with cloth bodies and bald delph heads and tin tea sets. Cap guns in holsters were the favourite for the boys, with the sound of caps going off all day. The Christmas pudding would have been made weeks beforehand. It was then left to hang in the calico cloth that it had been boiled in. On Christmas Eve, it would be taken down, the cloth opened, and the pudding revealed. Standing around the table, we each held a spoon to scrape the remnants of the sweet and spicy culinary delight remaining stuck on the cloth.

In spring, we gathered primroses and wild bluebells; in summer, we bathed in the sea; in autumn, there were chestnuts and mushrooms to be gathered. Halloween was celebrated with thick slices of buttered barmbrack at teatime. While my mother cut into it, we listened eagerly for the grating sound of her dagger knife touching the hidden brass ring. We played games of snap apple and dipped our heads in a basin of cold water to retrieve a threepenny piece. In winter, we made and threw snowballs with old woolly socks on our hands. Sliding for hours on the patches of ice without landing on our backsides was thrilling. If we fell and cut our knees, we were kissed better. We lived in an idyllic continuity that we thought would last forever. Alas, on one particular day, that blissful happiness was to be shattered. Life, as we had known it up to then, would never be the same. It was 29th January 1951.

I can remember it well because it was my ninth birthday. My parents had gone out in the evening to attend the funeral of my father's former landlady, Miss Marcella Mangan. Monica, who was nearly 16, was left in charge. Nicky and Helen were doing their homework. Malachy and Thomas were running, sliding and making noise up and down the front hall. When my parents returned, Monica complained of a headache. We were all sent to bed and told to be quiet. When Doctor Carragher examined Monica's eyes with a little torch, he came out to the kitchen to speak to my mother.

"I hope it's not what I think it is," he remarked gravely. "I'm going to call an ambulance."

My parents were panic-stricken. May and I, peeping through the bannisters of the stairs, could see my mother leaning on the high mantlepiece, her head bent between her outstretched arms, asking God what she had done to deserve this. The ambulance came and took our Monica away. It was the last time we were to see her smiling, beautiful face.

For three long months, my parents visited her in Cork Street hospital in Dublin. Children were not allowed to visit. We were told she had TB meningitis. It was the worst news possible. Each patient was allocated a number that would appear in a column in the Evening Herald newspaper under the headings of Condition Unchanged, Some Improvement, or if numbers disappeared, the patient had died. This period was traumatic for us. One or other of my parents went to visit the hospital each day or both of them on Sundays. Nicky, at 17 years old, looked after us and kept the range fire going. Helen got the shopping. May and I were delegated to go for the milk to Bell's farm at Hamlet Lane. Even though Jackie Campbell delivered the milk in the mornings from his horse and cart, by evening, the milk jug was empty. I clung tightly to May's arm on those cold and dark trips to Bell's farm. We sang and tried to speak Irish on the way.

In the afternoon of 25th April, while I was playing in the foundations of a house on the corner of Bath Road that had been left abandoned, Margaret Darcy came running telling me:

"Your Mammy and Daddy are home, and Monica's dead."

As I heard this dreadful news given so bluntly, it felt that I had been hit over the head with a heavy weapon. Although my parents had uttered the awful words that there "was no hope of a recovery," I was still totally unprepared for this news. I remember feeling bewildered. I knew that death meant gone to Heaven and that a hole would be dug in the cemetery and that you would never see that person again. I ran home. Uncle Nick's little beige automobile was parked outside our house. There was such a big crowd of people inside the house that I couldn't get past the front door. I could not get near my parents. They were surrounded by neighbours and relatives. Basie said I was to stay in her house and sleep with her daughter Mary. This was no consolation. I felt sick. Someone told me I was to be a good girl and to stop crying. This was impossible, as everyone else was crying. The next day, Drogheda Street was a sight rarely seen previously. Strange cars and vans were parked on either side of the street. My grandmother arrived from Drogheda in a big black Model T Ford taxi. George Harris, from Larkins' Garage in Dublin Street, arrived in a green, teak trimmed station wagon to take us to Cork St Hospital mortuary.

Aunt Peg lifted me up to see into Monica's coffin. I gazed in awe over the rim. My sister appeared to be asleep; so beautiful, so peaceful. Her dark hair hung on each side of her face. Her hands were joined. Red rosary beads were entwined between her pale wax-like fingers. Dressed in a blue satin habit, she looked angelic. Lined with white satin and trimmed with lace, the coffin seemed ethereal and not of this world. She had well and truly gone to Heaven. We followed the funeral cortège to St Peter and Paul's Church in Balbriggan. The Girl Guides and Boy Scouts formed a Guard of Honour at the church gates, as did Monica's fellow pupils and teachers from Loreto Secondary School. People came from far and wide. The crowds spilled out onto the road. I was still gripping Aunt Peg's hand as we entered the church. She tried to console me as she struggled with her own tears. I remember feeling a little proud and elated that this was all for our family.

These feelings quickly fizzled out in the weeks and months that followed. Even though spring had arrived and the daffodils were in full bloom, it was a depressing, dark and gloomy period for our family. In addition to having a black, felt diamond stitched to the sleeve of our coats to signify that we were in mourning, there was no music from the wireless, which was switched off for months, and the Sunday matinée at the cinema was also off-limits. Monica's illness and death due to tuberculosis was deemed contagious, and to see Monica's belongings – clothes, books, and personal effects – thrown in the fire by my mother was traumatising for us. My mother, at that stage, appeared angry and easily annoyed. Following my sister's death, my parents were heroic in their endeavours to make life appear as normal as possible for their remaining children. Their tears were shed in private and in prayerful acceptance of God's will. Even months later, if a particular song came on the radio, my father would suddenly jump out of his chair with tears brimming to make his way out to the back garden to examine the fence or to retrieve something from the shed. My mother kept busy as usual and suffered the loss of her beloved eldest daughter in silence. Sometime later, I learned that Monica's last word was "Daddy". That was the reason why he could never listen to Nelson Eddy's rendition of "When I'm calling you" whenever it was played on Radio Éireann's Hospitals Requests programme.

Chapter 7

EXTERMINATION

MAY EXPLAINED TO ME THAT Monica had died of TB meningitis and that as it was a "catching" disease, we would all have to be x-rayed. As soon as I heard the word beginning with x, panic and dread set into my stomach. Not knowing what this meant, I began to pray. I didn't want to die and go to Heaven. Some weeks later, we were kept home from school. An enormous white van arrived outside our front door. We climbed on board. There was another family already seated inside. We looked shyly at them, and they just stared vacantly back at us. Only their mother was with them, as their father had died from TB. We were on our way to the Jervo (Jervis St Hospital) to be x-rayed. I was sorry that I had not said goodbye to my friends, Mary Wherity and Niamh Kelly, who I believed I would not see again. I was convinced that we were all going to be X'd (exterminated) like those poor people in the war. We were contaminated and must suffer the same fate as the people who Hitler didn't like. Shivering in fear and keeping my thoughts to myself, I was unable to speak and whimpered, clinging to May. At the hospital, a hatchet-faced person in a white uniform kept telling us:

"Knickers and vest, knickers and vest."

Folding our arms across our bare chests, we soon realised that we were to leave our underwear on. Thinking that I was going to die, I wondered if I would go to Heaven? Certainly not. Hadn't I stolen a little ballerina doll from a music box belonging to Kay Brogan, had not always said my prayers, had even picked at a little sausage meat on a Friday? The list of my sins was endless. Each family member disappeared through a door leading to the torture chamber. They did not come out again. When my turn came, I was led through the same door to the cold X-ray machine and told to put my chin up on top and take a deep breath. My heart was breaking. The machine started to make a humming noise; I cried out loud to be so alone. But then, miraculously, I was alive. Stumbling out of the room through a different door to the one I had entered, I was reunited with my family and got dressed. It was such a relief to arrive back home safe and sound; I promised God that I would not do anything to offend Him again.

Chapter 8

BALROTHERY PRIMARY SCHOOL

Soon after this, my sister May and I transferred from St Peter and Paul's School in Balbriggan to Balrothery National School. This three-roomed school was three or four miles away from our home. The bus fare was three pence each way for each of us. So, in order to save money, my father acquired a second-hand lady's bicycle for May. We scooted up and down the street on it until we could peddle. I could not reach the saddle, but I bobbed up and down on the pedals. Sometimes May would peddle while I sat spread-eagled on the saddle.

Miss Connolly was my teacher, teaching second and third class. I missed out many days due to an outbreak of impetigo on my scalp. All my hair was cut off, and in addition to the itch and humiliation, a greasy, smelly pomade was rubbed on my head morning and evening. A woolly pixie bonnet hid the weeping sores night and day. A spoonful of Parrish's Food mixed with cod liver oil was administered to me daily. Bottles of this obnoxious concoction were handed out free from the local dispensary in High Street. This was not my only misfortune at that time. Having had cavities badly filled by the school dentist, it was decided, after the fillings fell out, that my five front teeth should be extracted. The fact that other pupils in my class suffered the same fate was no consolation. Us goofs and gummies waited months for partial dentures. This, of course, meant regular trips to the dental hospital in Dublin and a day off school. On these trips by train to Dublin, our first port of call was to Uncle Paddy and Aunt May's house down a lane to Frankfort Cottages off Amiens Street. Paddy was my mother's elder brother who had fought in Ypres during WW1. Aunt May worked in the Metropole restaurant over the cinema in O'Connell Street. She was able to take home the previous day's cakes, which would be deemed unfit for sale. We really enjoyed the special treats of cream buns and iced fancies rarely eaten in our household.

Some years later, when I was afflicted with a severe outbreak of eczema on my face and hands, salvation came from a visit to a pharmacist in Parnell Square called Mr Foley. At the rear of his chemist shop, he worked his powers, using a spatula to slap and slash various sloppy ingredients on a marble slab, filling a little round carton tub with a creamy pink ointment, and charged very little for his cure. A tour in Henry Street followed, including tea in Woolworths with a chance to spend sixpence on hair slides, school pencils and erasers.

My Uncle Paddy Hoey signed up with the Leinster Regiment of the British Army during WWI when he was just 18 years old. While at the same time, my mother's other brother Thomas aged 16, had enlisted with the Irish Volunteers to fight the British in the 1916 Rebellion, which took place in Dublin on Easter Sunday of that year. During the period leading to Independence in 1922, Thomas had been ordered to take part in raids of the homes of the gentry and aristocracy in order to commandeer rifles and ammunition, which these families kept in glass cases for hunting purposes. On one such occasion, young Thomas found himself on the property of his father's employer in Reynoldstown House, Naul, County Dublin. The raiders were disturbed by the old lady of the house who, in spite of his balaclava, recognised Thomas.

"I know you, Hoey," were the only words she uttered.

The boys made a hasty retreat, but the incident was enough to send Thomas on the run and into hiding for the rest of the Troubles. Retribution for his misdeed fell heavily on the Hoeys, however, and Granda Hoey was sacked from his job as ploughman on the estate. If that wasn't enough misfortune for the family, they were evicted from the rent-free tied cottage where they lived, which had been included in the wages. My mother was 11 years old then. She often recalled that time of hardship. All their worldly goods and belongings were piled up on a horse-drawn cart. She recounted years later that when the family was nearing Devlin bridge in County Meath, the Master of Reynoldstown – following them in hot pursuit on a galloping horse – offered to take my mother's brother, 12-year-old Francie as a stable boy. Granda proudly refused. He was unaware that his sacking as ploughman and his departure had caused the remaining farmhands to walk out on strike. He took them to Clarkstown in County Louth, where he found work. My grandmother was a truly remarkable woman who toiled in the fields, weeding and thinning swedes. Often pregnant, she suffered miscarriages and still reared her 11 children. She lost her husband to illness and two of her married daughters Lizzie and Bridget, during the same week in 1938. My grandfather died of natural causes, and Aunt Lizzy died aged 40, leaving five young children. Bridget, aged 35, died of complications, having given birth to her sixth child, a girl named Betty, three weeks previously.

When Uncle Paddy went to fight with the British Army in 1914, he was billeted for some time in Cobh, County Cork, while waiting for a ship to take him to England and then on to France and Belgium.

He wrote to his mother, asking her to pray for him and to tell his little brothers and sisters that he hoped the war would not last too long. He landed in France and was assigned the care of the horses, ponies and donkeys, which were widely used for the transport of infantry, supplies of ammunition and food. He was able to take his team of ponies, laden with supplies, up the hill to the soldiers at the front at the battle of Ypres in Belgium, under cover of darkness. His training as a groomsman in Reynoldstown was an asset to him as he could handle the animals to be very calm and quiet. On his return to Ireland after the Great War, he never spoke of the cold fear that must have strangled his guts in the trenches, nor of the sight of the dead and wounded. It never occurred to anyone to ask him either. Those who returned from these ghastly experiences were not accorded a hero's welcome. The Ireland he had left was now completely embroiled in the fight for Independence. Even though 122,000 Irish men had enlisted under the British flag and fought battles on the Western Front, with many deaths and casualties, those who returned were not shown any great admiration. Paddy never spoke again of his ordeal. Any post-traumatic stress he may have suffered was done silently, and he just got on with his family and his work for his remaining years. There was one consolation, however; he received an RSA pension for the rest of his life. In later years, whenever the brothers visited our house, they greeted each other by shaking hands. The war was never mentioned. They both lived into their eighties.

Mr Mullins was the headmaster in Balrothery National School and was as feared and respected as all the other teachers back then. As we dipped our rusty nibs in often dry delph inkwells, he stood with his back to the open fire warming his hands and his behind. A thick hawthorn stick was his weapon, inciting fear when used to keep the backbenchers awake by tapping it on his desk. A heavy slap on each hand with this instrument of torture for not knowing how to spell a word – which should have been learned off by heart during the previous days' homework – was both physically painful and humiliating. There existed a class divide whereby children of wealthy or professional parents were seated in the front desks while the less well-off usually occupied the backbenches. The reason for this was to give more attention to the pupils seated in front, thus promoting scholarships. Their parents could afford to support these in secondary school. Mr Mullins encouraged scholarships as this would inflate his ego, enhance his reputation and increase the school's popularity. Those at the back, packed in threes into desks designed for two pupils, were considered no-hopers despite some of them being more intelligent than those in front. These pupils were not worth bothering about. They would inevitably start work on the land or in factories aged thirteen or fourteen years of age. Firewood was collected by the back-seated pupils who were told to go out during class hours to gather bundles of kindling and sticks. The kettle was then planted on top of the burning heap and boiled for the cocoa at lunchtime.

Chapter 9

A DISASTROUS ADVENTURE

As no plastic bags or bottles existed then, we brought the milk, cocoa and bread to school in very rudimentary ways. The milk in old medicine bottles with ill-fitting corks often spilled in our school bags. Our books and copybooks would then smell until the end of term. Mary Rooney and Betty Connell were among my best friends. Jean Cunningham always had some money to spend on sweets in McNally's, so everyone wanted to walk home from school with her. In order to avoid too many hangers-on, some of us took a shortcut by crossing fields. There was a stream to cross. On one particular day, when we approached the stream, heavy rain had turned it into a rushing torrent.

"We'll have to jump over."

"You go first, Jean."

"Easy as pie," said Jean as she grinned from the other side.

When Betty and Mary had thrown their school bags, they leapt across like gazelles. Lastly, it was my turn. Preparing to leap, I flung my bag across. Alas, instead of landing on the embankment on the far side, it hit Jean's chest and fell into the fast-running water. I watched in horror as it disappeared downstream under the thick overhanging branches, weeds and hedges. Luck would have it that it was Friday. No school the following day. There would perhaps be a way of finding a solution and having time to concoct a story before arriving in school without a school bag and having to confront Mr Mullins. When we arrived at Betty's house, her mother tried to console me with a Mikado biscuit. Arriving home late was bad enough, but without my schoolbag and having to admit that we had not taken the proper road home elicited a right telling off from my mother.

Saturday passed. On Sunday, Mr Connell, Betty's father, arrived on his bike at our door with the sodden smelly bag. Cutting the overgrowth with a slash hook, he had spent all day on Saturday wading in the river, walking for miles searching for my school bag until he found it entangled in brambles that had prevented it from going any further on its watery journey. The pages of my copybooks resembled papier mâché, and the wrinkled pages of my book were stuck together. The stink of stale milk was not the only aroma that lingered on my bag and books until the end of term. No more shortcuts were ever made again.

Other smells remind me of my childhood. On washdays, my mother boiled tea towels and dishcloths in a great big pot on the range. The steam wafted to every corner of the house, filling our nostrils with the smell of cleanliness. Nothing compared to the whiff of fresh loaves when Jackie Shields arrived from Drogheda, opening the two back doors of his Lyons bread van outside our front door. I particularly recall with nostalgia, the smell of my father's glue pot bubbling in his workshop, of the cloths and rags he used for french polishing, imbibed with methylated spirits and linseed oil. I loved the aroma of my mother's cooking, and the smell of freshly washed up seaweed on the shore while listening to the sound of the foghorn warning fishermen of impending storms, or the sound of church bells ringing at midday and 6 pm to remind us to recite the Angelus prayers.

While in Mr Mullin's class, preparing to make my Confirmation, I sat the entrance exam to Balbriggan Technical College, which had just been built in Drogheda Street near my home. Miraculously, not only did I pass, but I also was among a few lucky pupils to be awarded a scholarship, which entitled us to free admission for the first-year enrolment instead of having to pay the yearly fee of one pound.

Chapter 10

1952

Monica had been in the Girl Guides. Two years after her death, I joined the organisation and was thrilled at last to be able to wear her brown leather belt. It was the last and only surviving piece of my lovely sister's belongings. An enormous brass buckle shaped like a shamrock glittered when polished. Buíon Réalt na Mara had been founded in Balbriggan by a local girl, May McGowan. She was the daughter of Joseph McGowan, proprietor of the Gladstone Inn in Drogheda Street. Meetings were held on Thursday evenings in Mrs McKeown's hall on the Square. Inspections were carried out by Captain Rita Carton. This meant our uniforms were to be immaculately presented, shoes polished, and hair and nails clean. The necktie could actually be used as a sling in case of a broken arm. Tuppence from each girl guide was collected as dues every week. Divided into patrols named after flowers or birds, each guide was under the supervision of a patrol leader and assistant patrol leader. Badges could be earned by acquiring skills such as cooking, first aid, singing, dancing and music. These badges were then proudly sewn onto the sleeves of our brown uniform. Marching drill was practised: left, right, left, right, fall in, fall out, about turn, until we resembled army cadets. Friendships were formed that would endure for a lifetime. In fine weather, we went on outings by train on Sundays to Laytown Beach, where we had a picnic and played games. May and Eileen Kennedy, Dolores Connelly, and Betty McMahon were my idols and always gave us good example.

On 19th April 1952, my mother gave birth to her ninth child – a girl named Claire. Everyone was delighted with this new arrival, who brought much joy and happiness to my parents and to her sisters and brothers. We wheeled her out and about in Malachy's pram, rejoicing as each tooth appeared, or a smile or wave of her hand. Some weeks after the birth, my mother told us to stay behind in the church after Mass. Watching her as she knelt down alone at the altar rails holding a lighted candle – while the priest reappeared in his vestments muttering in Latin to perform the ritual of "churching" – none of us understood what this was about. During this practice dating back to ancient times (performed among many cultures), prayers were recited, and a blessing was given by the priest – to give thanks for the recovery of the mother and that she be cleansed – before being welcomed back into the church. It was believed that childbirth and sexual activity deemed the woman unclean. This practice was discontinued after Vatican 11 Council (1962-65).

It was at this time that my eldest brother, 18-year-old Nicky, emigrated to England. The whole family went to the local train station to see him off. It was not unusual then for young people to go to Britain to work. He was accompanied by his friend Paudge Cullen. We didn't hear from him very often. As we didn't have a house phone, letters were the only means of communication. Some letters did arrive, however, and there would always be a five-pound note enclosed. Mammy must have missed him as dearly as we all did, but it must have been hardest for her as he was her firstborn, and he had always been so helpful and willing to carry out tasks such as skinning rabbits, bringing home fish, and cleaning out and lighting the fire. But we all missed his sideways grin, his intelligence and wit. He was the go-to person for answers while doing our maths, history or geography homework.

As my Confirmation day approached, I was excited to go to Dublin with Mammy for my new outfit. First stop was Clerys on O'Connell Street. As I tried on a gorgeous pink georgette dress trimmed with lace, I felt like Cinderella must have felt when the fairy godmother waved her wand. Mammy saw how happy I was. She let me have it. Then we selected a brown coat with a belt and a buckle. My shoes were brown leather with a strap across the instep. I was delighted and happy as it was the first time I had been dressed entirely in "bought" clothes. I could even smell the newness. All other clothes I had ever worn were either homemade or hand-me-downs. Some families in the street got parcels from relatives who had emigrated to America. These would contain clothes, comics and sometimes food or sugar lumps, which they would sometimes share with us.

We had very little occasion to have our photo taken as a Kodak box camera needed to be hired from Miss Wright's chemist shop for a shilling per day. In addition to this cost, a roll of film was bought to put into the camera. This would then be taken to the chemists to be sent away to be developed, with more money paid out on collection.

I remember very little about my Confirmation day except that the Bishop asked us questions on the Catechism, which we had been learning for years and were supposed to know off by heart. Each girl had a handbag for the coins anyone would give us on our special day. There were no big fancy meals in restaurants or hotels in those days, but we would make the journey to Dublin or Drogheda to show off our new clothes to our grandmothers, aunts and uncles. Taking the no 53 bus to see my paternal grandmother and Aunt Isla caused great excitement. They lived at 69 Church Road, East Wall, in a housing estate that had been built by Dublin Corporation on reclaimed land.

At Confirmation, it was normal practice to take the Pledge. This was a promise to abstain from alcohol, as part of affiliation to the Pioneer Total Abstinence Association (P.T.A.A.), which had been founded in 1898 by Fr. James Cullen, S.J.

The Promises and Pledges – taken by young people joining the Catholic Girl Guides and Boy Scouts, the Legion of Mary and the Sodalities – often led to vows in religious life or the priesthood. The culture of commitment to serve God and save souls was ingrained in our everyday rituals and practices.

It was during the summer of 1952 that Granny Mother came to stay with us for two weeks. She had arrived in her pony and trap. We had gone up to Coney hill on the Drogheda road to meet her and to climb into the trap for the jaunt of about a mile to our house. She always had bags of potatoes, vegetables, a bunch of dahlias from her garden, together with fruit and homemade brown bread. Her pony was left to graze in the field at the back of Dickson's Garage. Sadly, Granny Mother passed away on the last day of her visit. She was eighty years old. This was considered quite old then. She had not been complaining of any illness and just closed her eyes peacefully. My sister May had taken a cup of tea to her in the morning. I can still see, in my mind's eye, my mother kneeling down at the bedside, holding a lighted candle in Granny's hand and praying. Her wake was held in our house, and crowds came to pay their respects until a hearse came from Drogheda to take her there for her funeral.

Living in Drogheda Street during the early years of the 1950s seemed like the best place on earth. With not much traffic going past (on what was then the main Dublin to Belfast road) on GAA match days, we could still count carloads of fans on their way to Croke Park. We waved as they passed by with their county flags flapping out of car windows. Games of hopscotch, skipping, and marbles could be played in the street. At the end of April each year, encouraged by Mary Kenny, we started collecting pennies and sweet treats to be enjoyed on the first day of May when a large piece of hawthorn tree would be selected, cut, planted in a bucket and decorated with tinsel, ribbons and strips of coloured rags. A May Queen was selected. This was usually a young lady on the cusp of adulthood who showed signs of beauty and confidence. Songs were sung, games were played around the May bush, while sweets and lemonade were enjoyed by all the children of the neighbourhood.

This was also the era of the May processions. These took place in the grounds of the parochial house beside the church. Each Sunday during the month of May, parishioners paraded behind the clergy. A life-sized statue of the Virgin Mary was carried shoulder high by members of the men's sodality. The women's group, called the Children of Mary, wore long blue satin cloaks. A huge medal hung on a blue ribbon around their necks. The singing of hymns and the reciting of the Rosary could be heard at a great distance. Little girls who had recently made their first communion wore their white dresses and walked ahead of the procession, casting rose petals in the path of the congregation. Once a year, the big procession took place from the church to the town square, where an altar was erected. Benediction and Adoration of the Blessed Sacrament were conducted. Latin hymns and responses were sung by the choir and parishioners.

During this time, a mighty upheaval occurred in our household. Namely, the outside dry toilet at the bottom of the garden at the back of the house was to be replaced by a flush toilet. This tiny lean-to was being built outside beside the back door. As all the houses on our side of the street were getting this same upgrade, it involved a lot of digging and pipe laying. But only the hall in our house was being uprooted. A large trench dug by hand – with a shovel held by the perspiring Mr Dignam – appeared from the front of the house to the back. Entering or exiting, balancing tightrope walker style, extra care was necessary while walking the planks. However, it was well worth the inconvenience. In addition to the shiny toilet bowl and plastic seat, we now had the luxury of a sink with running water in the scullery. There was just one drawback to replacing the old loo. We no longer had a clear view of the street while using the new toilet. Whereas while seated on the old toilet, if the back door and the front door of the house were open, one could see as far as the other side of the street. This was a boon if one was in a hurry for the bus coming from Drogheda. A lookout would be appointed at the front door to see if the bus was coming over the hill at Bell's shop. This arrangement meant the lookout could signal if the bus were within five minutes of arriving. The would-be passenger would then run up the garden path in various stages of disarray.

Away… for God's Sake

Chapter 11

TEENAGE YEARS

WHEN I LEFT BALROTHERY SCHOOL in June 1955, the new Technical School in Drogheda St had just been built by the VEC (Vocational Education Committee), and this, for me, was an obvious choice. Near my home, it offered an opportunity to study shorthand, typing and commerce, which would provide female students with the necessary skills and opportunities to gain secretarial employment. Boys could study woodwork and metalwork. Other subjects were Irish, English, Home Economics and Maths. This was a marvellous chance for families who could not afford secondary education in private secondary schools, these being run by Religious Orders charging exorbitant fees each term. Only well-to-do professional people could afford to send their girls to be convent educated or their boys to be taught by the Christian Brothers or the Jesuits. Free secondary education was not introduced in Ireland until September 1966 by Minister for Education Donogh O'Malley.

Miss McDonald was my favourite teacher. Wiry haired, bleary-eyed and her false teeth clicking, she arrived each morning with the red indented trace of her hair net elastic on her forehead. She taught English and Maths. Mr Cody, the headmaster, was a strict disciplinarian. Boys and girls were segregated into different parts of the school. While the Christmas party was being organised, the girl pupils cooked cakes and tarts and made sandwiches. Everyone looked forward to the music and dancing. Boys crossed from one side of the room to ask girls to dance to the music of the fiddle, tin whistle and bodhrán. The easiest and most popular céilí dance was the Walls of Limerick, as it gave couples a chance to change partners often, to hold hands and to twirl with each boy. Spotting a very handsome fellow, I instantly developed a crush. I asked some people in my class if they knew who he was. His name was Eddie Mulvey, and he was from Garristown, a village about eight miles from Balbriggan. From then on, I was obsessed. I just had to find a way to attract his eyes. Paying particular attention to my appearance, I hung around Chapel Street corner so that I might see him arriving or going home on his bicycle. Eventually, we got talking. Besotted, I was completely in awe of his good-looking face and curly hair. He asked me to go for a walk after school as he was doing some extra study at five o'clock. We would have an hour together. I was thrilled. We headed for the beach and chatted as we climbed the path up to the cliffs. On that beautiful afternoon, we held hands and gazed at the horizon to where the mountains of Mourne sweep down to the sea. He gave me a photo of himself playing the accordion. When I arrived home at 5 pm, Fr. Corbet's car was parked outside our front door. He was in the parlour speaking with my mother. After the priest left, I got a right telling off. Fr. Corbett had taken no time in reporting that while walking on the beach, he had sighted me with a lad on the cliffs. This must have been humiliating for my mother to be told by a member of the clergy to rein in her daughter. Such was the power exercised by the Catholic Church; I was told in no uncertain terms to avoid the occasion of sin. I really did not understand what all the fuss was about, nor I did have any idea what that meant. Poor me, I was told by my mother that I was not to speak to him again.

However, soon after this episode, tragic love struck again. A drama class was introduced by Mr Jim Tunney, a new teacher of English. The reason for this was to teach us how to pronounce big words and to improve our elocution. A small vacant prefab in the schoolyard was available where we could rehearse a Passion play for Easter. Only certain boys and girls were chosen to take part. The lead roles of Jesus and his mother, Mary, were given to Harry Loughry and Eta Levins. I was to be Mary Magdalene. The part of Pontius Pilate was played by a big, strongly built 14-year-old called Tommy Connor. His deep-set eyes peered from behind thick lenses and black frames. But what a smile! We had already met some years previously on our way to collect the milk from Keeling's dairy farm. He had been eight years old then and was wearing his well-worn out First Communion suit, which had gotten too small for him. His family had come from Tipperary after the death of his mother. His father, a Sergeant in nearby Gormanston Army Camp, had met and remarried a local woman who became stepmother to his five children. No personal dialogue had passed between Pontius and Mary Magdalene during the rehearsals, but they happened to cross each other's path outside Spicer's Bakery one very dark evening. He had just been to Sheila Reynold's shop to get 2 pence worth of bulls' eyes. He produced the little brown paper bag from the pocket of his grey gabardine coat, and we exchanged pleasantries while we sucked on our bulls' eyes.

"I missed you in school today," were his first words to me.

"I have a cold," I stammered. "And a sore throat," I croaked.

We chatted for a while about school before he scuttled home through Convent Lane.

Rehearsals for the play continued, but no personal contact or words were possible between the male and female pupils. Luck, however, was on love's side. After choir practice at the local church, when Mary Magdalene came down the gallery stairs of the church, there was Pontius waiting for her with his little black cloth bag containing his altar boy surplus and soutane. As we walked home together, we had to be very discreet. In those days, friendships with members of the opposite sex were frowned upon. We had no idea why this was. Our knowledge of carnal desire was non-existent. With no one talking to young people about this, we only had a vague notion that something sinful happened between bad people. I certainly could see no harm in being friends and talking to and listening to another person who happened to be a very intelligent boy. Each time we met, we chatted about our families and of national and international news we had heard on the radio. Sharing our hopes and ambitions for the future, we laughed and enjoyed each other's company. Sometimes we took a detour around the beachfront. Winter turned to spring, and the play was a success. We then began arranging to meet for a chat on a regular basis. Each time we went for a stroll through Tanners Lane, round Clonard road and home by Chapel Street, we seldom held hands or touched except to thump each other when we disagreed about something. This went on for some time until one evening, while seated on a wall opposite the parochial house, he took my hand and told me he had something to tell me. My heart sank. I was sure he was going to tell me that he didn't want to talk to me anymore. He looked at me very seriously and said he loved me and that no matter what would happen in the future, he would always love me. I reached out and gave him a peck on the cheek and said:

"Me too."

We continued to meet at the church on sunny Sunday afternoons and head for our usual long walk. Time went on until one day, disaster struck. My sister Frances and I just happened to be upstairs looking out the front window when we sighted Tommy's pal, Francis Docherty, come running to our gate with an urgent message:

"There's ructions and war," Docherty shouted up to us.

Tommy's father had found out about our friendship. He obviously did not approve.

Docherty was breathless.

"Pontius told me to tell you, it's over," he yelled at me. The name Pontius was Tommy's code name.

"His brother Sammy is at Spicer's talking to your mother, so beware."

Panting and puffing, Doherty was still shouting while making a quick getaway.

My mother came in, but she wasn't angry with me. Addressing me in an agitated voice telling me to "steer clear of that lot", she obviously resented being apprehended by yet another male informing her of my behaviour. This was a Romeo and Juliet story. We were of the same religion and of similar working-class background, but Tommy was forbidden to speak to me again. School ended that summer. It was time for me to look for a job.

I never spoke to my friend again, nor did he look in my direction whenever we met. He obviously had been given a verbal warning, a hiding, or both, together with a lecture on the perils of keeping company with the opposite sex. Knowing how Tommy would have accepted the wishes of his father – and although I missed his friendship – I shrugged my shoulders and reluctantly accepted his rejection.

The drama class progressed, and we went on to act in two more plays: *The Rising of The Moon* about the 1916 Rebellion, with Ginner Carton playing the leading role, plus a comedy called *Hullabaloo*, in which I was given the part of a saucy maid. We even travelled to neighbouring village halls in Lusk and Garristown to perform.

The following September, the Gaelic League held a function in Smyths Hall in Convent Lane, at which a presentation was to be made to Tommy. A collection among members had been made, and a large black, leather-bound prayer book was presented to him. He was leaving his family and town to study for the priesthood in a Religious Order. He was heading to the Salesian monastery founded by Saint John Bosco. I attended, but I didn't speak or make contact with him. Knowing that he had washed his hands of me and that he had never mentioned his aspiration to enter religious life, I wondered if perhaps there had been pressure from his family. I also thought that he would be an ideal and suitable candidate for the theological studies involved. I hoped that he would be happy in his new life, which would enable him to pursue his ideals. Suspicions of the "do-gooder" who had informed his father of our friendship lingered in my mind. To this day, I am convinced that it had been a certain person, a member of the P.T.A.A. (Pioneer Total Abstinence Association), who we had encountered a few times on our walks, and even now can never look me straight in the eye.

Chapter 12

DANCES AND ROMANCES

My foray into the grown-up world of music and dancing began when I pleaded with my parents to allow me to accompany my sisters May and Helen to the "Hops" held in the town hall each Sunday afternoon from 3 to 6 pm. Music was provided by Tom Hagan and his band, with Charles Downes and Nicky Comerford on trumpet and drums. Quick steps, foxtrots, tangos, slow waltzes and the cha-cha were performed by very proficient dancers. No male even looked in my direction. Having tried to curl my hair and struggling with a stuffed borrowed bra, I gazed in wonder at the couples on the floor. Girls and ladies on one side of the room pretended to be not too eager to catch the eye of one of the lads lined up on the far side. My friend Niamh had been asked to dance by a handsome youth called Ollie Halligan. They performed the cuckoo waltz so well I resolved to get her to teach me. I decided to replace my white socks with nylon stockings before next week. My luck was in. Helen's friend Dolores Kiely discarded a laddered pair which I hastily repossessed. But not yet having a suspender belt, I had to make do with tight elastic garters. I never could keep the seam straight up the back of my leg.

At the next dance held in the town hall, I was less than happy when a gawky lad asked me to dance. My friends had nicknamed him Alan Ladd. He in no way resembled the famous actor. He must have fancied me because having invited me to the mineral bar, he asked if I would like to go to the cinema with him the following week. Reluctantly I accepted. As there was no way that I was going to be seen alone with him, I enticed Niamh to accompany me to the appointed rendezvous. We peeped out from around a corner to see if he was there. Sure enough, there he was, holding a brown paper bag outside Mrs Lawless's sweet shop in Bridge Street. Cold feet got the better of me, and we ran in the opposite direction. Years later, when we bumped into each other, he recalled that he was so annoyed at having been stood up that he had eaten all the Liquorice Allsorts himself in one go. Sorry to say, his appearance and dress sense had not improved with age.

During the first summer school holidays, I heard through a friend that there was a summer job available at Dublin Airport for a photographer's assistant. When I rang the number she had given me, a youngish male voice asked me to come for an interview. I washed my hair, and while it was still wet, I twisted pipe cleaners in my straight locks in order to get a curl effect. When my hair dried and the pipe cleaners were pulled out, I had a fuzzball and a fringe! I borrowed a skirt and jacket from my sister (without her knowledge) and off I went for the interview. The photographer's office was located outdoors on the tarmac under a concrete staircase. My interviewer was a young man with thick glasses and a mop of blond hair. His name was Billy O'Neill, and he was 19 years old. He was employed by a well-known photographer and had just completed the Leaving Cert at the Vincentian Fathers Secondary School in Glasnevin. He told me the job consisted of meeting each plane when it landed on the tarmac. I was to stand at the bottom of the steps, to hand out numbered cards to each passenger as they descended from the plane while Billy took their photos. They could then send their card complete with their money, names and addresses to Billy's employer, and their photo would be posted to them. He told me the job was mine and how much I would be paid per hour. Thrilled, I started the next day. Business was brisk. Passengers were delighted to accept the card. As air travel was expensive and very limited to a minority, those who could afford it were very proud to be photographed dressed in their Sunday best alighting from an Aer Lingus flight. I loved my job. Travelling by bus to and from the airport, I felt proud, sophisticated and grown-up. Alas, it was only temporary and finished at the end of the school holidays.

Billy and I hit it off from day one. We became great friends. Each evening, he accompanied me to the bus stop, gazing wistfully into my eyes. Sometimes he asked me to go to Dublin to an ice cream parlour. As I loved being treated to a Knickerbocker Glory in a tall glass, I went along. On days off, we met each other at Nelson's Pillar or under Clerys clock in O'Connell Street. I think he had a crush on me, but I didn't fancy him at all because, in addition to his looks being what I would describe as watery, he seemed to be from a different world than I. His father was deceased, his older brothers and sisters had left home, and he lived alone with his widowed mother in Artane. Having attended Handel's Messiah performed by the Rathmines and Rathgar Musical Society in Dublin's Gaiety Theatre, we ran panting and puffing to Amiens Street Station to catch the last train to Balbriggan.

On my 16th birthday, Mammy bought me a beautiful pink cardigan. I felt very grown up in this wool garment, which had been shop-bought and was not handknitted or a hand-me-down. Billy rode his bicycle from Artane to Balbriggan in freezing January weather to give me a bottle of 4711 Eau de Cologne and to take a portrait photo of me, which was duly framed and hung on our parlour wall for many years. I still have that photo to this day. When *South Pacific* was being shown at the Savoy cinema in Dublin, off we went to see this musical blockbuster. Having enjoyed it immensely, we raced to the station as usual for the last train. Back then, the train would stop at all stations from Amiens Street to Balbriggan. Billy alighted at Artane, while I continued on, with the train stopping at Howth Junction, Portmarnock and Malahide Station, with remaining stops at Donabate, Rush & Lusk and Skerries before reaching Balbriggan. It was at Malahide Station that I suddenly realised I was all alone in the carriage. Minutes passed. I could hear the station master banging closed the carriage doors that had been left open. A bewildered face appeared and peered in at me from the platform. The station master approached me.

"And what might you be doing here, my young lady?"

"I am on my way to Balbriggan," I replied, searching for my ticket.

"Not on this train," he bellowed, informing me that this was as far as the train was going and that the engine driver was about to disconnect his locomotive from the carriages. Panic set in. I was scared stiff. When he suggested I return with the engine driver to Dublin, there didn't seem to be much choice. I climbed aboard the locomotive and sat beside the engine driver. Chug, chug back we went in the direction of Dublin. I fingered my rosary beads, which my mother insisted I carry at all times in my handbag. Arriving at Amiens Street Station sometime after midnight, the place was in virtual darkness. Luckily, I had enough coins to make a call to Billy's landline to explain that I was stranded. His mother told me to take a taxi that she would pay for. Such a nightmare! I met Mrs O'Neill for the first time. She called the police station in Balbriggan, instructing them to inform my parents that I was safe and that she would send me home the next day. I was then ushered to her single bed. Leaning into the space between the bed and the wall while she tossed, snored, and turned her back to me, sleep was impossible. The reason for this cramped situation was obvious. Mrs O'Neill was not risking any nocturnal wanderings leading to hanky panky that could have occurred if she had allowed me to occupy the empty spare bedroom in the house.

Morning dawned, and I sat down at a well laid out breakfast table. While his mother was in the kitchen poaching eggs, Billy grinned over to me across the table and remarked:

"I would hope this occasion will coincide with the future."

Was this a proposal? Feeling nauseous, I immediately took a dislike to eggs. Things were getting a little too serious, and in the following weeks, I cooled it off and was happy that the friendship fizzled out before Billy got ideas of a more romantic nature.

Chapter 13

A REAL JOB

After my 16th birthday, a job became available in Smyco hosiery factory in Balbriggan. Made famous for the quality of its hosiery, Queen Victoria had her silk stockings specially made in this factory by Thomas Mangan during a period of over 65 years. John Wayne also wore his "Balbriggans" (long johns and vest underwear) in The Quiet Man film. Nylon stockings were now being produced by Smyth & Co in large quantities since the end of WWII and soon replaced silk hosiery altogether.

I started working in the stockroom. Quite a class divide existed between "staff" and "workers" – those who worked on the factory floor. Only Maura O'Malley and I worked in the stockroom. Considered neither staff nor workers, we muddled along, respecting both, under the supervision of Miss Babs Canning, who answered directly to one of the managing directors, Mr Ronnie Forsyth. Other office and administrative staff were housed away in another building. There were separate canteens for each. When Maura and I had a morning break, we were allowed to take a cup of tea and a chocolate-covered biscuit – which cost fourpence – in the staff canteen and only at a time when it was empty of office staff. Lots of girls with whom I had been to primary school worked in the mending room, the folding room or the dispatch department. Not being able to fraternise with them made me very uncomfortable. I spoke to them outside of work, at the Girl Guides or at choir practice. Occasionally, if Mrs Josie Levins in the folding room needed girls to work overtime, Maura and I were asked if we would like to come back to the factory at 6 pm to do some folding and packing. We jumped at the chance, and I have some great memories of hours folding delicate nylon stockings and putting them into cellophane bags. Of course, this also meant extra money in our pay packets.

Having a disposable income now allowed us teenagers a certain freedom to attend evening dances. The fireman's ball, the Garda annual dress dance, and the Scouts dance were greatly advertised and looked forward to.

I felt strongly at the time that I needed to better myself. My two older sisters, Helen and May, were working in offices: Helen in Stevenson's factory office at Sea Banks, and May in John O'Connor's insurance office in Dublin Street. Both were earning a lot more than I was, and they were able to contribute generously to the household budget.

Most of the staff and management at Smyth & Co. consisted of Church of Ireland members and were deemed a little different to us. This mentality stemmed mainly from the fact that Catholics were strictly forbidden to enter a Protestant church. My father, however, was an exception to this rule. Long before ecumenism was ever heard of, he had the tact and diplomacy to acquire a good working relationship with both communities. Often called upon by the Protestant community to work within the walls of their church, he regularly carried out repairs to doors, windows, pews and the steeple. He cultivated a high level of friendship in dealing with both clerics and the congregation. He certainly was ahead of his time regarding ecumenism.

Part 2

Chapter 14

ONE FATEFUL DAY

DURING MY LAST YEAR AT secondary school, when I was 15 years old, a visit to our classroom from a very gentle saintly nun called Mother Columba was to have a major impact on my future. Dressed in the usual black and white, she had a beautiful shade of blue material inserted into the veil that framed her face. Having travelled from Baldock, a town in Herts, England, she belonged to the Sisters of Mary and Joseph, a Religious Order founded in France, mainly involved with caring for women in prison and their children. Her aim was to recruit young girls interested in joining the Order.

I believed this was out of the question for me. I was of the opinion that one needed to have a calling from God and a rigorous commitment to the vows of Poverty, Chastity and Obedience, and to the Rule of the Congregation. I knew very little else. Some time previously, my long-time friend Niamh Kelly had departed to Bailieborough in County Cavan to enter the Presentation Sisters. We kept in touch even when she was later sent by her Order to Karachi, Pakistan. She worked as a teacher for many years before working permanently as a Presentation Sister in California.

In the past, I had accompanied Niamh on visits to her father's sister, who was a nun in Blackrock, Dublin.

I believed that in order to be eligible, a person had to have a large dowry. I began to wonder what this calling from God would be like. From then on, it seemed to be a gradual awareness of what God wanted me to do.

Mother Columba answered our questions, and I began to become interested in the particular work that was being done by the Order. It was an area of service that I had never heard of. Nuns in Ireland were either working in hospitals and education or went off to the Missions in Africa. I was intrigued and gave her my name and address, not thinking too much about the whole thing until a letter from Baldock arrived, and I started corresponding with Mother Columba. When I spoke to my parents, they did not take me seriously.

"Are you sure about this?" was my mother's first reaction.

"Well, I think so."

"It's a big undertaking, and you have to have a vocation. That means that God is calling you. Do you understand that? And that order of nuns being in France would mean you would be living in a different country and speaking a foreign language."

My mother's negativity went over my head. I also suspected that my parents might have secretly been happy at the prospect of having a nun in the family.

"Your Daddy and I think you are too young to be making such a big decision. Maybe you should wait a bit longer and see how you feel in a few years."

Her words went in one ear and out the other. But I waited a while longer anyway.

Some months later, on her next visit to Ireland, Mother Columba called to my home for a chat with me and my parents, who reckoned at 16 years old I was still too young, and that if I still felt inclined in a year's time, then it would be my choice. It was agreed that the situation would be reviewed again in six months when I would have reached 17 years of age. Reckoning their opinion to be fair enough, I decided to bide my time.

My contact with the nuns in Loreto Convent and their secondary school in Balbriggan was limited to a peep into the convent grounds through the hedge in Cumisky's field. I could see the nuns walking and praying in the garden. Day pupils and boarders played hockey in the sports field. Only the teaching nuns were addressed as Mother, whereas the Sisters were domestics in the kitchen doing all the cleaning, laundry and mending. The latter were the non-academic and those without a dowry. These Sisters sold bowls of roast dripping at the beggars' door. The idea occurred to me that this distinction did not exist in The Sisters of Marie Joseph in France. I saw that there was a class standard in Irish Religious Orders. However, I realised that such distinctions didn't seem to be applicable to this French Order, and so I began to be filled with joyful hope.

Months passed, and I prayed fervently, slowly coming to the conclusion that a vocation or calling from God was not going to be a flash of bright light or a heavenly apparition. There would be no sign similar to that which Saint Paul had encountered on the road to Damascus. No, it was a growing attraction to religious life. In retrospect, was this an opportunity to travel, to escape from an overcrowded household and the monotony of working in Smyth's factory? My dalliance in romance could often have been compared to a damp squib. Attending the local hops, I still enjoyed dancing the tango, foxtrot and slow waltzes. Dressing up and experimenting with my older sister's clothes and make-up, and gazing at my reflection in the full-length mirror on the front of my parents' big mahogany wardrobe, I often imagined myself being a film star or at least resembling some of the swanky ladies who strode up to the front seats at Mass on Sundays. Swimming in the sea and sunbathing with my sisters and friends in summer was also one of my favourite pastimes. I knew that I would miss all this.

I began to read some poetry and books on spirituality, especially the works of Canon Fulton Sheehan. I had joined the local Altar Society and arranged the flowers in the church. As a member of the local Legion of Mary group, I prayed for the salvation of souls and the return to the Church of members of Jesus' flock who had lost their way. I spoke to the chaplain of our school. We chatted about faith, the liturgy and the sacrifices entailed by the vows of poverty, chastity and obedience. I started to believe the loss of marriage and motherhood would be compensated by the apostolate of saving souls and that service to God would be fulfilling.

As a member of the local Girl Guides, I tried to live a good Catholic and Christian life. At home, I felt a little cramped, although, by this time, my brother Nicky had left home permanently when he had gone to England. We didn't hear from him too often as we did not have a phone.

Whenever I spoke to my parents about my interest in this French Order of nuns, although they kept repeating that I was still too young, they did not object or seem opposed. Mother Columba wrote regularly, and in early June 1959, I had decided to travel to Baldock in England for a trial period. There was very little discussion in my presence about my impending departure.

Chapter 15

BALDOCK, HERTS

An airline ticket arrived for me, and I packed whatever clothes I possessed in a small suitcase. Prior to my departure, I had met another girl named Breda in Dublin for coffee before she travelled to the convent. It was my first ever flight. I was so excited. I hardly said goodbye to my family, and they did not seem too concerned. I got the impression they must have been thinking I would be back soon enough. Looking out of the small window on the Aer Lingus plane, I felt no regrets as I watched the Irish coastline receding. Having no idea how long it would be until I would catch a glimpse of it again, I remember feeling proud of myself, and above all else, I wanted my parents to be proud of me. It had always been believed in Ireland that to have a priest or a nun in the family was a great honour, that it would be a direct link to God and that parents of large families would then have a daughter or son who they no longer had to worry about. They would be safe and secure for the rest of their lives in God's care within the sanctity of the Church.

I was met at the airport in London by a sparrow-like little woman called Mrs Shepherd, who took me to lunch at Liverpool St Train Station before our journey to Baldock. I remember how bland the peas and mash tasted. I felt sick but did not complain.

My first impression of St Joseph's Convent was that it was a most beautiful red brick building. It was built to a French design in 1907 to accommodate members of the Soeurs de Marie Joseph during a period of religious upheaval in France. By 1959, in addition to being home for many small orphans, it was also a rest home catering for a number of elderly female paying guests, most of whom were bedridden or confined to their first-floor rooms. Several steps led to the front door. The grounds were beautifully kept, with flowering rose bushes plentifully planted between neatly trimmed low box hedges bordering the pathways.

Feeling instinctively that I would be very happy during my short stay here, the door was opened by a large nun with a broad smile. I was enveloped in a massive embrace and kissed on both cheeks. This demonstrative French greeting was totally new to me. Ma Mère, as she was both addressed and referred to, led me to a parlour where I was greeted by three other girls who were dressed in their own clothes. They were all Irish; Breda and Katie from Dublin and Mairead from County Waterford. We were to be called aspirants, and we would help to look after a group of small children, mostly Greek, who were being looked after here. We were entrusted to look after these children while the nuns had their meals.

This was to be a time of discovery both on my part and on the part of the nuns as we began our mutual acquaintance. It was easy and interesting to look after the children each day from midday to 2 pm. There was a large outdoor playground and an indoor playroom. An enormous old Pye radio in the playroom provided us with a link to Dublin. Whenever we managed to twiddle the knobs to get Radio Éireann, we listened to Hospitals Requests, which was my father's favourite lunchtime programme. My room on the third floor overlooking the backyard was small but brightly decorated. Instead of feeling privileged at having so much space, I felt very lonesome being in a room all to myself for the first time in my life. I missed my sisters. I had no trouble sleeping and would have preferred to stay in bed longer in the mornings, but Sister Yvonne passed by our doors at 6 am, shaking her bell vigorously to wake us up for Mass. The same bell called us for lunch and evening meal. As every minute of each day was mapped out for us, we didn't have much time to feel sorry for ourselves. We were allowed to write one letter home per week. Days were regimentally structured: Mass, breakfast, chores, lessons, lunch, childminding duties, more lessons and study of the French language, evening prayer, supper and recreation. Chores consisted of cleaning and polishing floors, dusting, watering plants. There was a rota of spending one or two mornings per week in the laundry, mostly helping to fold sheets and towels. During recreation, we played ball games outdoors or knitted and sewed while chatting with the nuns. Lessons were exercises in French reading and writing.

I fondly remember trips to Whipsnade Zoo, to Cambridge and to the market towns of nearby Hitchin and Stevenage. The summer months in 1959 were sunny and enjoyable. We chatted and laughed amongst ourselves, and loved every minute of every day. My ultimate aim at this point was to progress to the next stage, which was to set off to the Novitiate in France, where I would spend the first six months on probation as a postulant before being accepted as a novice. This would be followed by twelve months of learning and training for eventual profession and taking vows. During this training period, both the Congregation and the novice would have the opportunity to get to know each other. This was my goal as I waited in anticipation of the day I would depart to the Continent. Each aspirant would travel alone at different times in order to make room for new arrivals to Baldock from Ireland.

The nuns were wonderful. It was always a pleasure chatting with them. Mother Columba was the Reverend Mother Superior, Mother Euphemia (referred to as Ma Mère) was a retired Reverend mother and the most jovial, kind and lovable person. There was Sister Vincent from Waterford and another French sister called Sister Christine, who was the cook.

They belonged to Soeurs de Marie Joseph des Prisons, founded in France in 1841. The Motherhouse and Novitiate of the Order were situated in the small town called Le Dorat, nestled in Haute-Vienne province in the Massif Central. The blue strip inserted in the nuns' veils had been introduced by the foundatrice in order to bring the colour of the sky to those imprisoned in the dark dungeons.

We tried our best to speak, read and write in French. It was expected of us to eventually become fluent. Ma Mère, being a native speaker, conducted our daily lessons. As I had never studied it as a school subject, I struggled at first during these lessons. The first thing we learned was to say the Hail Mary and the Our Father prayers. This enabled us to participate in reciting the Rosary each evening with the nuns in their chapel situated on the first floor. Soon enough, I learned to count and say the days of the week. Gradually I started to understand what was being said to me but found it impossible to reply in the language.

Chapter 16

THE JOURNEY

AFTER TEN OR TWELVE WEEKS as an aspirant at St Joseph's Convent in Baldock, I was given the good news that I would be departing to France shortly. I let my parents know that I would be travelling to the Novitiate in September of that year, 1959. I was happy and excited at the prospect of progressing another step. My parents arranged to come to London from Ireland to see me off. I suspected that while they were in London, they'd also wanted to make contact with my brother Nicky – who we had not seen for nearly six years and from whom we rarely heard.

A big suitcase was packed for me. It was much larger than the one which I had arrived with in Baldock. Ma Mère explained that she was sending some things to the Sisters in France.

Before my departure from St Joseph's Convent in Baldock, I was given a huge pink corset, which I was to wear on the journey. This item of clothing was a total surprise to me. It consisted of two parts, which were joined at the back by thick laces tied all the way from top to bottom. The front fastenings could be described as tortuous hooks and eyes made of steel; rigid "bones" were stitched in at two-inch intervals around the bodice and made bending or turning nearly impossible. The only time I had previously seen a corset was when Mammy would "loosen her stays" at the end of a hard day's work. This piece of torture with which I was confronted on the morning of my departure seemed to have no purpose whatsoever. I had no shape that would distinguish me from a young male. I weighed less than 50kg, and this excruciatingly painful piece of underwear restricted me whether I sat, walked or just stood still. Wondering whether it was intended as some form of penance to test my mettle or just as a means of holding up my thick stockings, I thought that it was perhaps to keep my body from slumping forward. I put it on and carried on as best I could. It reached from bust to thighs.

In the moving train, as I headed on the short journey from Baldock to London, accompanied again by Mrs Shepherd, I was very uncomfortable. My ribs and lungs seemed to be dangerously compressed. Breathing became difficult, but I kept smiling. Arriving at London Bridge Station, my heart skipped a beat when I saw my parents waiting there. Much to my surprise and pleasure, Nicky was there too. We hugged and chatted for a while before the train I was to take to Newhaven for the ferry to Dieppe departed. I felt really happy that Nicky had agreed to go back to Balbriggan with my parents. It eased the sadness of saying goodbye. I did not tell them that it would be at least ten years before I would be accorded a visit to Ireland. This fact had been explained to me beforehand, and I didn't have the heart to tell them. Mrs Shepherd ushered me on to the train and made sure I was seated beside a nice respectable, mature lady.

The train journey to Newhaven passed without incident. I was looking forward to the boat journey to France and seeing the country where I was to spend the rest of my life. I lugged the big suitcase onto the ship and sat down uncomfortably with the bones of the corset stabbing me in the ribs. I started on the packed lunch Ma Mère had given me. While eating my sandwich from the brown paper bag, a big green apple rolled from the soggy bag and made its way to the other side of the deck. Having chased it, I was unable to bend down to retrieve it due to the corset, which by this time felt like a suit of armour. Red-faced and sweating, I accepted the apple, which had been picked up by a little boy and given back to me.

The sea voyage took about four or five hours, and when the coast of France loomed ahead, I queued with the rest of the passengers to disembark from the vessel. At the bottom of the gangplank, there were some people waiting to greet their relations or friends. I was immediately struck by the sight of two gentlemen embracing and kissing each other three times on the cheek. I was shocked and even more confused when I noticed everybody else was doing it too.

The train journey from Dieppe to Paris would be the last leg of this journey. I was alone in a country where I didn't know the language. Feeling tired and nervous, I tried to put on a brave and confident face, avoiding eye contact with the other travellers and wishing this ordeal over. I had very little knowledge of anything about France. My only insight had come from reading *A Tale of Two Cities*. I had been intrigued reading about the French Revolution, especially the story of Marie Antoinette being beheaded while Madame Defarge sat knitting at the foot of the guillotine. Signposts at train stations or words on billboards that I caught a glance of from the speeding train appeared incomprehensible and strange.

With the suitcase in the overhead rack, I settled in or tried to settle into my seat. As the call of nature beckoned, I stumbled and wobbled to the toilet. Ah, as I sat down, a light bulb moment struck. What if I could free myself for a few blissful minutes of this awful tightness around me? So, off the corset came, and I felt such a relief that there was no way I was going to put it back on. But what could I do with it? How could I dispose of it? It wouldn't fit in the bin, and if I left it lying on the floor, the next person waiting outside to use the loo would probably run after me with it. There was only one thing I could do.

Sliding back the very small window, I pushed the cursed cause of my suffering out into the wind of the speeding train. Whether it could be seen by the rear passengers or whether it landed on a hedge, I did not care. My stockings began to fall around my ankles. These I took off and put in my pockets, and away I went back to my seat. I smiled to myself, feeling free at last.

Chapter 17

ARRIVING IN PARIS

HAVING TRAVELLED FOR A WHOLE day, as the train pulled into Gare St Lazare in Paris, I was delighted to see two Sisters with the distinctive blue strip in their veils. I was to stay overnight with the community within the walls of La Roquette prison.

Fortressed, this enormous building resembled an ancient walled city, with each corner having a rounded turret. An imposing edifice in the 11th arrondissement occupying a large portion of four streets, the entrance door had a small iron-barred window out of which a face appeared when the nuns rang the bell. We were admitted and proceeded through a few more doors until we found ourselves on a black cinder-covered walkway to the nun's building. There were about twenty-five or thirty nuns living within the high walls of the prison. Some were housed in the convent pavilion, while others occupied cells within the prison. Everything seemed to be blackened by acid rain.

Inside the nun's building, which was called the Community, I was shown into a small parlour where a meal of thick vegetable soup on a tray awaited me. I was then invited to join the Sisters at their evening recreation. I met two English Sisters and one Irish nun. Mère de la Croix, the Mother Superior, appeared and greeted me with an

Irish welcome. She was from Dunboyne in County Meath. It was impossible to guess what age she was. After a somewhat exhausted sleep and breakfast, I was accompanied to the railway station of Montparnasse for the train to Le Dorat. From that point on, I was alone. I was to change at Poitier. Having no idea at this stage of any sense of direction except that I was heading south, I settled into my seat, hoping for the best.

I was happy enough to travel alone and enjoyed being on the train without the corset. The French countryside was beautiful, and the towns we passed were interesting. The townhouses and buildings were unlike those in Irish towns. White-washed with Tudor-style dark inlaid beams, shuttered windows and very few front gardens, these dwellings seemed to be of a long-ago era. I was happy and curious to be heading to a new life. Feeling that this was my chance to better myself, I hoped my family would be proud of me. Funnily enough, I didn't feel lonely or homesick. My enthusiasm made up for all that I had left behind.

Chapter 18

LE DORAT, HAUTE-VIENNE, FRANCE

IT WAS A GREAT FEELING to know that I had arrived at my destination. The Mistress of Novice's assistant, and Breda, who I had known in Baldock, were at the station to meet me. To my great relief, they loaded my heavy suitcase onto a wheelbarrow. We chatted as we walked towards the Motherhouse and Novitiate. It was a beautiful sunny evening, and I marvelled at the old buildings, the trees and the abundance of flowers everywhere. I arrived in time for supper and recreation, then evening prayer in the chapel. Hearing the Sisters chanting the Sacred Office was spellbinding. The echo of their voices reciting in a high-pitched tone in Latin was inspiring. It really was another world. There were about forty Sisters from the Motherhouse, together with twelve novices and six postulants. Nervousness and wonder mingled with a temptation to cry left me weak at the knees, and I hoped that my bladder and bowels would not let me down.

On arrival, I had been given a black tunic-like dress together with a little black lace mantilla, which I held onto my head with hair clips. Proud as punch, I was now a postulant. I had a new title. I was to be addressed as Mademoiselle Catherine. I would be a postulant for six months before I would be officially received into the Congregation and given the black habit and white novice veil.

The daily routine consisted of being woken up at 5.15 am. The dormitory had recently been refurbished into cubicles, which afforded us some privacy. In each cubicle, there was a single bed, a hand basin, and a white curtain at the entrance. Very often, when the shutters on the dormitory windows were opened first thing in the morning, the sight of the glorious sunrise was awe-inspiring. We were to be ready, washed, dressed and lined up at the chapel door before 5.45 am, for meditation, the chanting of Matins, Lauds (which was part of the divine office recited in Latin) and Mass. The Motherhouse and the Novitiate were separated by the large chapel. The postulants and novices entered by one door, and the elderly sisters and those visiting from other houses entered from the other side. Instructed to keep our backs straight while seated, leaning on the back of the seat was deemed a weakness in a young person.

Oh Gosh, I really wished for breakfast during that first morning Mass. Having fasted since the previous evening meal, my stomach rumbled, and I felt sick. When breakfast time eventually came, we ate in silence. We each had our own spot for each meal. The reason for this was having our own little drawer in the table in front of us, where we had our own cutlery, a weekly portion of butter in a ramekin dish and a linen napkin. Usually famished, I quickly devoured the piece of French baguette bread allotted to me. Tearing it into pieces and dipping it into the bowl of milky coffee, I longed for the taste of a thick wedge of crusty batch loaf, slathered in butter, the memory of which lingered each time I sat down for breakfast in this faraway land. No cups of sweet milky tea were to be had either. Until I got used to the taste and smell of coffee, I missed the smell of our family teapot bubbling on the range.

After breakfast, we each had an allocated area to clean and dust. Shuffling along the floors, our feet firmly planted on "les patins" at all times, novices and postulants moved slowly in silence – in a zombie-like way. The patins were dark foot-sized pieces of tweed or felt, with several rectangular layers stitched together. Their purpose was twofold. Floors were being dusted and shined, and the noise of footsteps eliminated. Everything worked like clockwork. Breda had been assigned as my "guardian angel" to show me the ropes and help me navigate the timetable during the first few weeks. She did her best to explain everything to me. This was not an easy task, as speaking time was limited. We had no watches. The bell being our only means of knowing the time, there was no way of anticipating how much leeway remained before the next exercise. Everything looked spotlessly ship-shape. There was no talking allowed unless absolutely necessary. Mornings progressed very fast with lectures and lessons in the French language. As the class consisted of Irish, French, Dutch, Spanish and English postulants and novices, we struggled to communicate and were encouraged to speak French. I had no idea what anyone was saying.

Lunch consisted of fish, chicken or beef with vegetables, cheese, yoghurt or fruit. I was very surprised that each day we had a carafe of red wine on the table, with each person having a half tumblerful, topped up with water. An hour of recreation followed. Weather permitting, we played volleyball outside. On rainy days we stitched or darned our clothes or stockings. Lectures by the Mistress of Novices followed. Seated in a semicircle, we tried to be attentive, but it took a great effort to stay awake. Sitting opposite to us, Mère Mathilde was a beady-eyed, owl-shaped little nun. Her mouth seemed beaklike. She had a continual drop from a constant sniffly nose. Her voice was barely audible. Not understanding a word, some of us nodded off, to be nudged in the ribs by our neighbour. If this happened in the chapel, it was a kick in the shins. After about three months, I finally started to understand the language.

At 4 pm each day, a welcome break led us to the refectory for water, dry bread and surprise, surprise, some squares of dark chocolate. This kept hunger at bay until after another visit to the chapel – this time for evening prayers together with part of the divine Office called Vespers. Chanted in Latin, this evening prayer of thanksgiving and praise marked the beginning of the rule of strict and complete silence, which would be imposed until after Mass the following day. Not only was speaking forbidden, but doors also had to be opened and closed noiselessly, and walking had to be on tiptoes. Supper consisted of a weak vegetable soup, salad and fruit. Each one of us took turns at reading aloud during meals until Mère Mathilde tapped on a little bell in front of her to signal the end. These readings were religious writings of saints and scholars. Not understanding much in the beginning, but as time went on, I realised that these readings were based on the lives of the great Saint Teresa of Ávila, Thomas Aquinas or Saint Thérèse of Lisieux, among others. The laundry, kitchen and food stores were in the Motherhouse. Novices were delegated to collect and deliver from these areas. This would entail a short walk through a beautiful garden surrounded by a low wall. The height of the wall created an illusion of being near the street, but alas, on the other side of the wall, there was a 15ft drop to the road below. If one had occasion to meet a professed Sister in the garden, it was strictly forbidden to speak to said Sister. In retrospect, perhaps this rule was to deter the older nuns from influencing the novice by discussing the negative aspects of religious life, or to discourage Irish compatriots from forming friendships.

Away… for God's Sake

No world news ever filtered into this cloistered environment. Politics, progress in research, changes in fashion or music never reached us. There was no TV, radio, newspapers or phones. Strangely enough, I never felt hemmed in or curious about what was happening outside of the high walls. The feeling of belonging to this family seemed secure and magical. I remember feeling exquisitely happy. Ambition to progress and please the superiors spurred us on and helped us to strive for the level of perfection required. Greater detachment, humility, and holiness were constantly included in lectures and at one-to-one meetings with the Mistress of Novices. Whenever I entered her office, she indicated a low stool where I was invited to sit. This meant that while she peered downwards at my upturned face, I peered upwards into her moist nostrils. This tête-à-tête usually took place monthly, whereby each postulant or novice would be interviewed, assessed, and their progress evaluated. These conversations consisted mainly of spiritual matters such as bible studies, assessment of our devotion and closeness to God, and how we felt about dedication to the rules of the Congregation. Any shortcomings or misdeeds noted by her or reported to her by others were pointed out, and a reprimand ensued.

The months passed, during which time we prayed, learned and laughed too. Outings on Sundays for a long walk were a real bonus. Instructions to avoid eye contact with members of the public obliged us to keep our eyes lowered, and hands remained up our sleeves until we reached the outskirts of the village. Two by two, heads bowed, we shuffled caterpillar-like in silence until we emerged into the open countryside. When a signal from the accompanying Superior enlightened us that speaking was allowed, songs erupted on lonely side roads where there was no traffic. Chatting and laughing, we turned our heads to the wind, and sun, skipping and swinging our arms.

Having been confined and restricted to a strict routine during the week, whereby it was against the rules to talk unless it was absolutely necessary, I always felt deliriously happy and content on these outings. *It's a long way to Tipperary* was known by all and was our favourite tune. Whenever we had a picnic by a lake or a stream, it felt great to be alive and out in the great outdoors. Conversations about our family back home were discouraged, as were "particular friendships" with any of our colleagues. This was repeated often in lectures and talks given by superiors.

This brings to mind the weekly Mea Culpa ritual, which took place after lunch on Fridays. At what is called the Chapter in monasteries and convents, a section of the Holy Rule of the Order is read. Each member then publicly confesses and repents their misdeeds. Mère Mathilde, or occasionally Mother Superior General, would sit in front of us in the large day room where we spent most of our time studying and listening to lectures. Each one of us, in turn, knelt to ask forgiveness, and penance was given to us for transgressions and omissions committed during the week. Speaking or making noise during the great silence was most often confessed. Dropping and breaking anything was deemed major. During one particular Mea Culpa session, I had difficulty keeping a straight face and refraining from laughing out loud when one of the novices knelt and asked penance for having been vain – looking at her reflection in the brass ball of the newel post at the bottom of the stairs. As there were no mirrors, it was considered a point of vanity to gaze at one's reflection in a windowpane or any other shiny surface. The purpose of this exercise was to instil the virtue of humility, which would take us nearer to resembling Jesus – who welcomed the meek and humble of heart. Penance would be given by the presiding superior to each repentant before these red-faced miserable wretches rose from their knees to return to their seats. Depending on the nature or gravity of the misdeed or omission, penance ranged from reciting a rosary to eating a meal kneeling on the ground.

Chapter 19

THE BICYCLE

WHEN SISTER LAETITIA AND I were delegated to weed the gravel paths in the Motherhouse, we had to retrieve some gardening tools from a shed. On opening the door, lo and behold, we spied an old rusty black bike, covered in cobwebs leaning against the wall. Sister Laetitia looked at me and smiled. No words were exchanged. Without hesitation, she grabbed the bike and off she went at full speed. Without any air in the tyres, she pedalled furiously. I could see the badly chopped strands of her hair when her veil went up in the air like a parachute. When it was my turn, I hitched the skirt of my serge habit into my knickers. Racing with bated breath on this old bicycle through the gravel paths between the trees, sheer joy and exhilaration left me breathless. I wobbled, and before I could get my feet on the ground, the bike and I fell sideways into a small young pear tree laden with blossoms. No injuries were sustained, but oh dear, the pear tree was lying flat on the ground under me! Hoping to have been unseen, we returned the bicycle to its dark, forgotten space and quickly completed our chores in the remaining time allotted to us.

"Maybe Mère Superior think the wind blew the poirier to ground," my Dutch companion managed to utter in broken English.

No such luck. Days passed, and Friday's Mea Culpa loomed. Fear and guilt tore at my guts. Mother General entered the room with a sweeping flourish, wearing her usual stern countenance.

"Mes filles," she intoned, "It has come to my notice that one of our fruit trees has been sabotaged. Hopefully, the perpetrator will admit to the damage."

I knelt down and contritely uttered the two words which would appease my conscience. "C'est moi."

Glancing up from the floor, I could see Mother Thèodore's nostrils twitching. Her beady eyes narrowed, and her lips parted to utter the required penance:

"Eat your potage on your knees from the ground for the rest of the week," she scowled.

I never rode a bicycle again until years later.

Our chaplain, Monsieur l'Aumônier, celebrated Mass each morning and heard Confession monthly. Confession day was regarded with dread. He didn't understand English. Translations for sins such as laziness, envy, disobedience and jealousy were searched for in the dictionary. If we could not find it in a dictionary, we asked one another for a list of sins in French. I often choose the easiest to pronounce just for something to say. And if, after examining our conscience, there was no sin, well, one had to improvise and enter the little dark confession box to wait for himself to slide the grid back before we read off our misdemeanours from a scribbled piece of paper. This was a nightmare. Being very dark inside made it impossible to read my prepared confession. This meant leaving the door ajar to allow a chink of light to creep in and therefore risking being heard by those kneeling outside, causing them to titter.

I must have been speaking loudly, or I must have looked bewildered whenever I was spoken to because, one day, out of the blue, I was informed by the Mistress of Novices that I was going to Limoges to be examined by an audiologist. Chaperoned by Sister Pierre, we travelled by train. I was thrilled to be going on this return journey to the town renowned for its porcelain. I wasn't aware that my hearing was impaired in any way, but it must have been noticed that I was either intellectually challenged or that my hearing was not up to scratch. I never got to know what the outcome of the hearing test was. But the fact that I was not sent home on the grounds of ill health led me to believe that I was acceptable on both counts.

During Lent and Advent, writing our regular letter home to our family was not allowed, nor did we receive any mail. Our letters were to be written before Advent or Lent. All letters written were to be left open for censorship by an anglophone Superior. Incoming mail from our families was opened and read before being distributed. My letters to my parents were always cheerful, newsy and telling them how happy I was, how enjoyable life was in a convent in France; the weather, the food, and of course asking how everyone was getting on in the family: anything except how I was really feeling. My mother's letters were fantastic and greatly looked forward to. We prepared well for the feast of Our Lord's birth. Christmas hymns and carols were rehearsed as well as a pageant. New decorations were fashioned from scraps of tinsel or coloured paper. The crib and Christmas tree were erected, and table decorations were made from whatever greenery, berries or blossoms could be found in the garden. It was a truly joyful and enjoyable occasion.

The rule of no mail or parcels being distributed during advent was strictly adhered to. A parcel containing tea bags and chocolate that my mother had sent for Christmas was not given to me till after

Christmas. This annoyed me, but when a pot of hot water arrived from the kitchen to steep the tea bags and share the precious brew between the other Irish novices, this special treat consoled me somewhat. Novices from various other countries were not interested in tea, so this meant more whoops of joy from the Irish contingency at every sip of the precious liquid.

Reading my mother's first letter after New Year's Day 1960, I learned the good news that my eldest sister Helen was engaged to be married. She had known Ray Fullam since she was a schoolgirl and had been keeping company with him since she was sixteen years old. I had been ten years old then and used to see Ray arrive outside in his little red Morris Minor. This was delightful news. It brought back to memory the evening Helen had asked me to watch out for him and to run out and tell him she would be late, that he was to wait for her further up the street in case my mother would see him loitering outside our house. She was absolutely not to find out about these goings-on. I had crept out and had approached the car door when a heavy hand grabbed me from behind and pulled me away. It was my mother who opened the car door and told him in no uncertain terms that if he wished to wait for Helen, he could do so inside the house! She could then have a good look at this curly-headed stranger and quiz him as to his intentions, his integrity and background.

Chapter 20

RECEPTION OF FIRST VEIL

A FEW DAYS AFTER TURNING 18 years old at the end of January 1960, I was called to Mother Mathilde's office to be informed that I would be officially received as a novice into the Congregation. On July 2nd, I would be given the holy habit and the white veil that I would wear for twelve months before taking yearly temporary vows. I would also be given a new name, which would be chosen for me. I was delighted with this promotion and was proud that I had climbed another step up the ladder.

When the day of my formal reception into the Congregation arrived, the assistant Mistress of Novices dressed four other girls and myself in long white silk dresses and placed a flimsy lace veil on our heads. Our hair had been washed and curled with strips of calico so that we would appear worthy of our Divine Bridegroom. As this figurative ritual was not explained to us, the notion of being a bride of Christ did not particularly appeal to me at all. I could not imagine Christ having so many brides! But I went through the ceremony of laying prostrate before the altar and promising to obey the Holy Rule. This followed by much singing, while we newly received novices were ushered backstage. There, a huge pair of scissors was produced, and our hair was chopped very short – following the custom of tonsure dating back to medieval times.

We were then given the black serge habit and white headdress. This consisted of a white starched linen contraption called a guimpe (through which the face would appear), which was tied by tape at the rear. Then came the piece covering the forehead and knotted at the back. The white novice veil was then pinned on top. This last piece covered arms and shoulders and reached down in a v-shape to the lower back. When presented with a small cloth bag containing a cat o' nine tails, shock and horror engulfed me. Gasping in fear and dread as the Mistress of Novices explained that this instrument of flagellation was to be used in private, on bare flesh in the attic, I was instructed that this ritual was to be kept a secret from the younger postulants and must never be spoken about to anyone. Allowed to chat and laugh during a special meal laid out for us in the refectory, I felt proud and delighted to have made it this far.

From then on, I had a new identity. Now known as Sister Marie de Lorette, my past life was beginning to gradually fade as I fought hard to erase memories of home. Thoughts of my family, Balbriggan, or Ireland, were constantly cast from my mind. Striving for continued contentment, I threw myself into prayer and contemplation and to study the French language assiduously. I had not chosen the name, but I liked it because it sounded good. It reminded me of Loreto school and the convent near my home. It is also the name of the town Lorette in Italy to where it is believed that angels transported the house of Jesus's mother, Mary.

As the seasons rolled by, the year as a novice seemed short, and much was still lacking in our preparation for the task ahead as professed Sisters of the Prisons. I would soon make my temporary vows, which would be renewed yearly. These were just as binding as perpetual vows usually made after five years of temporary vows. I continued to enjoy life in the Novitiate; sunny hours were spent picking the blackcurrants and redcurrants in Monsieur l'Aumônier's big garden at the rear of his house on the opposite side of the road. In fine weather, recreation was taken outdoors, playing volleyball or topping and tailing large quantities of green beans when in season.

When my sister Helen and her fiancé Ray decided on the date of their wedding, they immediately announced that they would honeymoon in Paris and would include a visit to Le Dorat. Thrilled and excited, I had no idea of how it would unsettle me. Neither did I know or care how Mother Mistress of Novices felt of this intrusion. After all, it was unheard of in those days for families to be able to afford travel by train or airfares. No one else had had family visits. On the day they arrived, I was allowed to sit with them in the parlour. The time allotted was very short, but as they were staying in a local hotel, they would be back again the following day. This did nothing to alleviate my tristesse. I wanted to spend more time with them, but I was instructed that the usual timetable of the Novitiate must be adhered to. I wept in secret before their departure and even more when they had left.

Occasionally, we visited La Providence, a house near the Novitiate run by two Sisters of the Congregation. Caring for a group of small children entrusted to them by the Dept of Justice, the Sisters had created an atmosphere of love and homeliness where the little girls appeared happy and healthy. Removed from various backgrounds, ranging from parents who were in prison, in hospital or deemed unsuitable due to alcohol or drugs, this oasis was now their home. The establishment was also a place where during WWII, Jewish children had been hidden during searches by the Gestapo. Those same two brave Sisters had risked their lives moving their little protégées from wardrobe to coal bunker to closet.

I was once sent to the Motherhouse to help Mère Agathe prepare the rooms for Sisters arriving from various community houses to take part in the yearly retreat. The rooms were made spick and span, polished and dusted. Beds were made up, and a chamber pot placed under each bed. Mère Agathe was very particular about the latter objects of convenience - plain white delph ones for Sisters and flower-patterned china for the higher-ranked Reverend Mothers.

My father Richard Byrne

My mother Catherine Byrne née Hoey

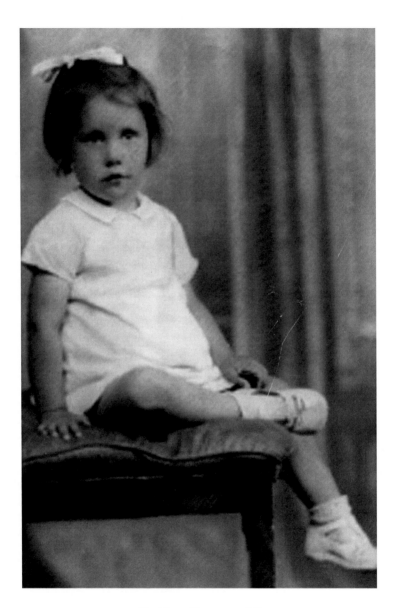

Kathleen Byrne aged 3

Above:
Best friend Niamh Kelly
and Kathleen overlooking
Balbriggan Beach, 1950

Right:
Kathleen and Niamh Kelly
in the Girl Guides

Kathleen at sweet sixteen

At the convent in Baldock 1959 before going to France.
Back: Breda, Margaret. **Front:** Kathleen Byrne, Kathleen Hutton

The first veil I wore as a novice

Kathleen with May during her visit to Paris

Becoming Soeur Marie de
Lorette at my profession

La Roquette prison in Paris

Le Dorat, where my religious life began

Gardening in Basses Pyrenees, France, 1965

Looking after the children at Christmas in Bordeaux, 1964

John and Kathleen on their wedding day before
heading off on honeymoon in 1971

My sisters, Claire and Frances, and my nieces and nephews enjoying sunshine at the old bathhouse in Balbriggan

My brothers and sisters (Left to right) Malachy Byrne, Claire Sweetman, Frances Monahan, Helen Fullam, May Mc Keon and Thomas Byrne

My nieces and nephews at the wedding
of my niece Fiona Kavanagh

John, Kathleen, Joanne, Catherine and Katelyn in 2012

My family in Fiji at Joanne and Mark Naish's wedding

Chapter 21

FIRST PROFESSION

As THE YEAR AS A novice progressed, we learned about the Holy Rule of the Congregation, the ritual of the Holy Office, which must be recited daily, and the obligation required to observe the vows of poverty, chastity and obedience. Poverty consisted of not owning anything. All our needs were met; anything we required must be asked for. This vow required economical use of property and materials. This included not wasting food or electricity, mending our clothes and not complaining of cold or heat. Any gifts given to us would be deemed superfluous to our requirements, and it would be at the discretion of our Superior whether it was to be shared, given to charity or kept for our own personal use. Incidentally, during this time, none of us was ever sick or had an ailment. Permission had to be sought to use the shower. Toothpaste and soap had to be humbly asked for. A box of clean white rags was available in the dormitory for monthly periods. Made of coarse heavy linen and pinned to underwear, these left the groin chafed and painful. After use, these rags were then to be deposited in a linen sack that was taken to the laundry, washed and returned for reuse.

In relation to Chastity, I knew very little except that this vow meant I could never marry or have children. Sex, or the absence of which, had never been spoken about, either during my childhood or adolescence. I had a vague notion that it involved male and female anatomy. When I was about eleven or twelve years old, a girl who lived beside us in Drogheda Street said to me one day that her granny had told her a secret and that if she repeated it to me, I was never to tell anybody. She proceeded to say that her granny told her about a girl in Duleek who was not married but who had a baby.

"She went into long grass with a lad who put his mickey into her mickey, and the result was a baby that came out down below," she said conspiratorially.

Well, I gave my informant a slap on the face. I was horrified.

"You're a liar, and your granny is a witch," I cried.

Trying to put this out of my head, the enigma still bothered me. I tried to figure out a way of getting more information. Too ashamed to ask anyone of my own age, one day as I sat at our tea-table waiting for my mother to deal out the thick slices of loaf that she was chopping with her dagger knife, in the meekest and most innocent voice, I blurted out:

"Mammy, could Elsie Duggan and Jimmy Sharky make a baby if they were not married?"

These two were a local spinster and bachelor in middle age who were in no way connected. My father spluttered into his tea, and the rest of my brothers and sisters fell silent. Quick as lightning, the dagger knife came down on my wrist. I can't remember whether it was the sharp or blunt edge!

"Don't you ever speak like that again in this house. And go up to bed. NOW!"

So off I went, hungry and none the wiser. I never dared mention bodily contacts between males and females again.

As the day of my vows approached, both ignorance and innocence prevailed. I had a vague notion of "sins of the flesh." In my mind, this could be gluttony, sloth or any number of sins, even laziness. I had heard the expression "carnal knowledge" but didn't really know what it was. Love in a relationship was never mentioned. I associated erections with tombstones, signposts and flagpoles! In fact, the whole idea of chastity was to be pure and a virgin. Anything remotely the opposite was sinful, bad and dirty and even thinking about it would be sinful. The words sacrifice and mortification surfaced many times in lectures and retreats. In an ambience void of television, magazines, or influences of the world outside of our cloister, I really did not ponder much on the subject.

Obedience to the Rule of the Congregation slipped into our everyday lives. I knew that this would entail being dispatched after Profession to any of the prisons or youth centres where I would take up my duties. I would have no choice as to where that would be. Each placement would be on a temporary basis, even if it was to last for years. One would have no fixed abode and could be expected to be shifted around the country for any number of reasons. Regulations would have to be adhered to, and any particularities would have to be accepted. Timetables in every community would be different. Anything requiring a dispensation from this would require permission from the Mother Superior. Punctuality was expected to be rigorously maintained. With every minute of every day in the year being mapped out, I would no longer make decisions or decide what I would or would not do.

Looking back at my childhood, these vows did not appear harsh. I had previously owned very little, had been kept strictly in the dark in relation to the joys of physical love, I was unaware of what the vow of chastity would deprive me of, and had I not always lived in obedience to my parents and the Church?

My parents and my Aunt May travelled to Le Dorat for my Profession on a beautiful day in July 1961. The ceremony was joyful with lots of hymns, followed by a special meal with my parents looking happy and proud. It never occurred to me at the time that it must have meant scrimping and saving and making sacrifices to be able to afford the expense of such a trip. They enjoyed the excitement of flying for the first time to Paris, where they struggled with the lack of communication and strange food. Before their departure from Le Dorat, we were informed that I would be going to work at the Roquette Prison in Paris. This made it possible for them to visit me at the Sisters' residence within the prison walls before they returned to Ireland. I didn't have much free time with them in the city, but we did some sightseeing; we visited Versailles and Marie Antoinette's Little Trianon. On one occasion, when I was unable to accompany them, my father got lost when he emerged from a public toilet from the opposite side to where he had entered and failed to see my mother and my aunt waiting for him around the corner. Fortunately, help came from a gendarme who stayed with him until he was found again.

Chapter 22

STARTING WORK AT THE PRISON

Raw, nineteen years old, newly professed, and totally naive, but oozing enthusiasm, I was introduced to the rest of the community. There were about 35 Sisters of all ages and experience working here. The two English Sisters I had met on my first visit, Sister de la Compassion and Sister Christopher, were very friendly and welcoming. Sister Compassion had worked in the prison library for 20 years. Childhood polio had left her mobility impaired, and she got around with the help of a cumbersome surgical boot. This meant outings to the outside world were very few for her. Sister Christopher was very gentle and loved to plant flowers in the border of a grassy patch beside the cinder path.

Very early on, I could see the other Sisters smiling or casting their eyes to Heaven whenever the two English Sisters endeavoured to join in the conversation or attempted to express their views in the French language. Accompanied by Sister Andrea on my first day, I entered through the many doors leading to the workshop occupied by the group of detainees for whom I would be responsible during the day. Here I would be the sole surveillant during my hours on duty. The roll call was made from a raised wooden platform where I sat overseeing the group. "Oh, dear!" I sighed. A sea of faces stared at me. The names of these women were impossible to pronounce. Blushing, stuttering and with my voice shaking, I struggled until one kind detainee came to my rescue to read out the names while I watched each one raise a hand. I prayed that said hand belonged to the person named and hoped no one would notice my red face and laboured breath. To my relief and surprise, each one sat quietly and continued their work. About 30 women of all ages and nationalities sat on long wooden benches at tables laden with cardboard boxes containing their belongings. Their task consisted of threading string into labels, whereby each detainee could earn a monetary reward on her release. Alternatively, earnings could be spent by ordering supplementary food or toiletries. Earnings were accounted for on paper by the outside entrepreneur who supplied this labour. Meals served in this workshop had to be fetched from the kitchens by two selected from the group. Great ladles of porridge, soup or mash, and whatever was on the menu on that day would be distributed by the Sister in charge into the tin receptacles kept by each of the women in their cardboard boxes. Spoons were the only cutlery allowed as knives or forks could be used as weapons. Sister Andrea explained that she would be back to relieve me at 4 pm. That meant another six hours on duty. I would be responsible during that time for opening the door out to the yard for recreation. Having heard the older Sisters refer to certain detainees as "les femmes sales" (dirty women), I was perplexed. They all appeared to take their personal hygiene seriously. It took quite a while for me to stumble onto what the Sisters meant. It was their way of labelling prostitutes and lesbians. Not a very Christian attitude on the part of those consecrated to God! This attitude of certain Sisters towards these "lesser mortals" began to niggle at my mind and would continue to cause me to question our role in the prison.

On sunny days the women lay outside with eyes closed, imagining that they were on the Côte d'Azur getting a tan. With Edith Piaf the most popular singer of the day, strains of *Je ne regrette rien* could be heard all over the place, sung of course by one or other of the detainees. They sometimes came up to me on the rostrum to chat about their problems or the reason for their incarceration. The particular group I had were mostly first-timers: illegal immigrants, backstreet abortionists, prostitutes, or those caught for fraud and embezzlement. Most of the group were French, with some Spanish, a few Asians, all struggling to communicate. Many tried to speak a little English when they heard my accent. As I was also struggling with the language, needless to say, I was unfamiliar with the vulgar vocabulary of these ladies, especially when they called each other names. It was a constant problem for me and caused great mirth when I appeared embarrassed or not to have understood.

Being a detention centre, those within were deemed innocent until proven guilty. None of these ladies already incarcerated for various lengths of time had yet been on trial. They were being interviewed regularly by their lawyers and were allowed visits by their families at allotted times during the week. Mme Le Sage was the longest inmate who had not yet been tried and sentenced. For seven years, she had been in the same cell. She had collected posters and photos, artificial flowers and various knick-knacks with which to decorate her abode. She was highly educated and intelligent, and was respected by the other detainees. She readily admitted to anyone who would listen that she had walked into a Parisian restaurant, shot her husband and his mistress at point-blank range, having no remorse whatsoever.

In the absence of any form of lay security, the fact that the Sisters in charge were able to maintain law and order was nothing short of a miracle. The incarcerated women – a lot of whom had had little or no previous contact with religion – were amazed and often in awe of the nuns who looked after them all day, every day. They showed respect to these visions of goodness and probably thought of us as heaven-sent. We endeavoured as much as possible to treat them fairly and with respect. This was most likely the reason why the Ministry of Justice allowed the situation to continue since the Order was founded in 1840. The vow of poverty meant that we, as individuals, were not receiving a salary, but financial payments were obviously being made directly to the Motherhouse in Le Dorat. This money was then redistributed to the various community houses of the Order dotted around France, including in each of the penitentiaries in Paris: La Roquette, St Lazare, the Dépôt at Préfecture de la Police, and at Fresnes where a prison hospital was also serviced by members of the Congregation who were qualified nurses.

At this particular time, Charles de Gaulle was President of France. The Algerian War of Independence from France raged during this period. French Algerians who opposed independence and carried out terrorist acts were arrested and arrived at the Roquette prison in large numbers. Political prisoners involved were either members of the Front National de Libération or the OAS, which was a terrorist paramilitary organisation. Protests by sympathisers of the OAS were taking place in the streets of Paris. Many arrests were made – of partisans from both sides of the conflict – with those incarcerated at the Roquette prison segregated in the political wing. However, there were many others sympathetic to the cause of the conflict also distributed into various workshops. Discussions, debates and arguments broke out with much shouting and clenched fists, both in the workshops and in the yard. As each group had a separate enclosure, voices sometimes rose high enough to be heard over the other side. The Sister in charge often reported the mayhem to Mother Superior, who would send her assistant to admonish the unfortunate Sister responsible for the group where the row had broken out – for "lack of authority". She would bang on the rostrum with her heavy six-inch key and roar, "Silence, Mesdames".

The miscreants feared Reverend Mother's assistant, calling her "oeil de lynx" (eye of the lynx). For major transgressions or unruly behaviour, a detainee could be deprived for a certain time of goodies they ordered from outside. To be deprived of cigarettes was the worst punishment, and the culprit could be seen later in the yard trying to puff at a lighted twisted piece of brown paper. A lot of bartering took place. Cigarettes and sweets were swapped for a little Nivea cream mixed with biro ink, to be used as blue eye shadow. The regrowth length of roots of those with bleached hair indicated how long they had been detained (approx. 1 inch per month), so great efforts were made with lemon juice and even with Parazone bleach. The results were often hilarious – with hair in shades of green, or a red-raw scalp. Attempts made to cut each other's hair with blunt scissors, which were very occasionally supplied by the outside entrepreneurs for short supervised periods during the day, produced peals of laughter from spectators or tears from the unfortunate victim.

News trickled into the women from the outside world by way of family visits. This included gossip of one or other's partner's or husband's infidelities. Any such information triggered rants, rages and tears from the women inside. Tales and tittle-tattle resulted in grief, frustration and anger. Life, however, was not all gloom and doom.

Hope of an early release or acquittal was often expressed by someone asking for our prayers. Some spoke often of their children, their lovers or husbands and resolved to reform their lives. They had access to social workers, and appointments were made to speak with them.

As the days and months passed, I settled in quite well to the routine of life in the community and work on the coalface. All the working Sisters occupied a cell identical to those occupied by the detainees. Mine was situated on the first floor, in the same corridor as the ladies who were entrusted to my care. It was a single cell identical to all the others. It contained a single bed, a bowl and a jug of water on a small table, a chair and a shelf to hold my few belongings. There were no other furnishings. A thin curtain on the barred window accorded some privacy. A crucifix and a picture of Mary, Joseph and Jesus on the wall were the only decorations. When not on duty until the late shift, I made my way at 6 am to one of the turrets where, with other Sisters, we waited for a small door to be opened by Sister Germaine. This allowed us to exit the main edifice and gave access to the community pavilion for morning prayers, Mass and breakfast. Afterwards, we returned to relieve the Sister who had been on night duty and who would have by now opened the cell doors of the detainees on her corridor. The inmates would, by this time, have tidied their beds and emptied their slop buckets. They then proceeded to descend in single file to the workshop for breakfast at 9 am.

This routine was sometimes interrupted by pleasant outings. I sometimes had the privilege of accompanying a senior Sister to the nearby boulangerie for large quantities of French baguettes. This was a wonderful treat, as was the outing to Mass in the nearby parish church when on night duty. Before going on night duty, a flask of coffee and a sandwich could be collected from the nun's kitchen, followed by a short rest in my cell until the appointed time of my first round of inspection. These short periods of reflection gave me some respite in a cold, dreary, gloomy environment. Headcounts were to be carried out three or four times nightly, the times of which were altered each night. A small hatch on each cell door allowed us to count the sleeping beauties within. We had to make sure that it was actually a person in the bed and not just a pile of clothes under the blanket. Cells accommodated three people or a single individual, but never two. This seemingly was to avoid a row erupting where two could injure or kill one another, whereas if there was a third, this person could intervene, call for help or, in the event of a tragedy, be called as a witness.

A key had to be inserted into a meter on the wall in each section to record the time the round of inspection was made. This particular key was attached by a chain to a chronometer, which we carried across our shoulder. At a certain small window, the sight of the illuminated Eiffel tower could be glimpsed in the distance. What a contrast this was; it reminded me that there was another life out there where people were dining in restaurants, mixing with their loved ones, and feeling free and happy.

The monotonous daily grind was occasionally relieved by outings on Sundays in the beautiful city of Paris. The sun seemed to be always shining. Three or four of us Sisters regularly made our way by metro to Notre-Dame Cathedral, the Sacré-Cœur Basilica or other churches of interest. This was something I could mention in my letters home. It would have been inappropriate to mention the homesickness, tiredness or the sheer loneliness of living a life of separation from the outside world of freedom or of being deprived of any real contact with people. Friendships were strictly forbidden amongst our colleagues in the community. Conversations were always of a jovial nature, with no real exchange of information about one's past, our families, or news of any kind. The chapel of the Miraculous Medal in Rue du Bac was a favourite place to visit. It was there that Saint Catherine Labouré had received the design of the medal during a vision of the Virgin Mary. This chapel was part of an enclosed convent, and the entrance from the street was through a huge imposing portal leading to a courtyard where pilgrims who had been cured over the years had left their crutches and mementos. The saint's body could be seen intact, enshrined in a glass case on the high altar. She appeared to be sleeping. Crowds of people of all nationalities came to pray and assist at Mass in this atmosphere of quiet contemplation. I enjoyed the aura of peace and tranquillity, feeling that with the saint's body visible, there was a connection to heaven.

At no time during my sojourn at the Roquette did I doubt my vocation. This was what God had called me to do. I endeavoured to carry out my duties and to observe the rules of the Congregation. I prayed alone, and also when I was supposed to pray together in the community. Each morning and evening, I thanked the Lord for having called me to do His will. The spiritual training as novices in Le Dorat was called to mind regularly. The virtues of humility and detachment were put to practice constantly, and sacrifices were made as the months went by.

The seasons came and went, and during the summer of 1962, I had a wonderful visit from my sister May who had come to Paris on holidays with two of her work colleagues. Oh, the joy of seeing her again! We were able to walk to a nearby park, chat and have coffee and cake in a café. It was such a joyful reunion with just the two of us going over times past; I could not contain my happiness and the sheer joy of being with her. I remarked on her beautiful clothes, and her hair permed in the latest fashion. She told me about her romances and heartbreaks, that she had a great job in Mulcahy and Sutherland Insurance offices in Dublin and that my parents were well and that they were still talking about their trip to Le Dorat and Paris. She gave me all the news of Nicky, Helen, Malachy, Frances, Thomas and Claire. I tried hard to not let all this news unsettle me, but this was difficult. I could only imagine what changes a few years had made to them. I did not have any photos of my family. As we were constantly reminded of the need to be detached from people, this would have been frowned upon. May did, however, have a camera to take some photos of us together to show to people back home.

When it was time for us to say our goodbyes, I kept the tears back until she was gone. A stiff upper lip would be required at the evening meal in the community. I was just about able to follow the conversation at the half-hour recreation which followed. There was no place to hide the feelings of desolation and utter stomach-churning sorrow until darkness fell and I could retire behind the door of my little cell. It took some time afterwards to recover and to get back on track.

Back in the everyday job, life continued with its challenges and joyful moments. The words of Jesus, "I was in prison, and you visited me" (Matthew 25:24 - 40) were a constant reminder of what I had to do, and this was a great source of strength both mentally and physically. I was improving spiritually and was happy that I was becoming fluent in the French language. Always in good health, I was eating well and sleeping adequately. The shift work in the workshop with the detainees was interesting. There were quite a lot of departures and arrivals among the women as they attended court and were either acquitted, in which case they didn't come back, or they were sentenced and moved on to another prison to serve out their sentence. Each evening a new consignment of detainees arrived in the Black Maria from the Préfecture de Police. The Sister in charge of new arrivals had the task of meeting the unfortunates at the front entrance, where she would witness each one being searched and identified by lay wardens or surveillants. She would then sort them out by category: first-timers, recidivists or tramps. This last category was made up of homeless vagabonds who roamed the streets, begged and slept on park benches. Content to live like this in good weather, in winter, they would make nuisances of themselves to the public and police in order to be arrested and readmitted to the Roquette where they would get a dry bed and three meals daily. They were well known to the Sister in Charge, who arranged for them to be deloused and showered before admittance. This job was done by another Sister, who then escorted them to their cells. On one such occasion, Sister had assigned a new arrival to a cell already occupied by two ladies. A short while later, these ladies caused such commotion in the cell that two Sisters were required to remove the newcomer. While undressing, it had been discovered that this person was male. He was quickly dispatched to La Santé Men's Prison.

Alas, alas; eventually, my vow of obedience was tested in a major way. Mother Superior summoned me to her office. She assured me that she was pleased with my work and progress but that I would be going to Bordeaux to work in Nazareth House, also run by the Congregation. Within a few hours, my few belongings were packed and, still reeling from this quick departure, I was on the train south.

Redeployment at short notice was not unusual within the ranks. Reasons were not given, but it was common sense to believe that vacancies occurred in the various houses of the Congregation due to the death of older sisters, old age, sisters leaving the Order for personal reasons, or of being expelled due to their behaviour or unsuitability. There was a belief that if a glass tumbler was broken while washing up that the person responsible would soon be shifted. This was pure superstition and rarely happened. There was no choice in the matter of where or when the changeover would occur, and it was expected to be received as God's will and with joyful acceptance. The vow of obedience had to be observed without question.

Chapter 23

BORDEAUX

ARRIVING AT GARE SAINT-JEAN RAILWAY station, my first impression was that Bordeaux was a bright and cheerful place. The city, situated on the River Garonne, which flows into the Atlantic on the west coast of France, is steeped in history with lots of beautiful architecture. On that first sunny day, I remember feeling excited and happy to be starting a new chapter in my religious life. A cool breeze reminded me that I was now not too far from the sea. I knew that the climate in the southwest, being neither too warm nor too cold, would be a relief from the sometimes sweltering heat of Paris. I was delighted to be met by an Irish Sister, a little older than I, who hailed from County Monaghan. We took a taxi to 239 Rue St Genès, the address where I was to spend some of my happiest years. Reverend Mother was from County Waterford. Although tall and imposing in stature, she was very gentle in nature. She smiled often and had a wonderful way with the Sisters and children. Twenty-five other Sisters made up the community, each one actively engaged as house mothers, in administration, or the general run of the establishment. Lay women who lived in or out were employed in the kitchen. Adèle, the cook, lived in with her Spanish husband, Moise. Moise drove the bus belonging to the Sisters while also acting as gardener and odd job man.

Nazareth House occupied a large site on the corner of Rue St Genès and consisted of several buildings, a large chapel and the Sisters' residence. A concrete yard separated the children's living quarters from the schoolrooms. The whole area was surrounded by a high wall, except at the entrance to the chapel from the street and a small door at the parlour where an elderly Sister acted as receptionist and sentry.

The children's ages ranged from three to sixteen years old, and they were divided into three groups: Les Petites (3–7yrs), Les Moyennes (8–12yrs) and Les Grandes (teenagers). Another small group consisted of some children taken from each of the groups who were given separate quarters because of special needs. All these children from various backgrounds were living in Nazareth House for different reasons. Most of them were wards of court, having been removed from parents found unsuitable by the Ministry of Justice. Many had been abused, had been living in drug and alcohol afflicted family homes, were orphans or children of prisoners. Two or three siblings of the same family were among them. Their mental and physical conditions were apparent by their aggressiveness, their sadness or attention-seeking behaviour. It was hard work at first dealing with these beautiful, boisterous little girls. But with consistent, caring attention, they were very receptive to their surroundings. Although the environment was institutional, it gave them a certain amount of security and safety in a warm and clean environment. A fairly strict routine in a structured framework accorded some stability in an atmosphere where they could cope and learn to accept their circumstances.

I was delighted to be assigned to the youngest group of children. This group occupied Le Nid (The Nest). Meals were served in the dayroom. During school hours, the room had to be cleaned and tidied. Outside of school hours and on weekends, this was where we lived, played, sang, danced and enjoyed craft activities. The dormitories were on the first floor, with each group having their own washroom and walk-in linen cupboard. My bedroom was on this floor. This was a small oasis where I could sleep, write letters and house my worldly belongings, which were very few.

Although I was not informed of individual circumstances, the certainty of their past suffering and trauma was obvious as I became more acquainted with the group. There were exceptionally sad cases among the children. Little Nicole, an only child, had witnessed her mother being murdered by her father. He was serving a life sentence in prison, but due to a terminal illness, he was in the prison infirmary. I had the task of taking her to see him there so she could bid him a final goodbye. He passed away shortly after her visit, and I had to inform her of his death. She was seven years old. Siblings Catherine, Monique and Josie's eldest sister, who had been looking after them, died in a nearby hospital of skin cancer aged 29. Émilie had a heart condition, and as her house mother, I was responsible for her medication. Each child was unique, but it was difficult to treat them as such as they were part of a group, and it would sometimes be necessary to referee disputes without taking sides or showing preferences.

The work of looking after the children's emotional and physical welfare was greatly assisted by the presence in each group of a student from the l'École d'Éducatrice Spécialisée. Each of these young adults stayed for about six months. Marie France was my assistant. We worked well together. I learned a lot from her theories and practical skills. She ironed all the clothes and bed linen for our group. The linen room was kept immaculate, and she had wonderful ways of entertaining the group. She taught me how to crochet and corrected my French grammar in a kind way.

Classrooms within the establishment meant that the pupils were educated in situ. Lay teachers were employed, and schooldays were kept as normal as was possible in an enclosed environment.

The Sisters' refectory and common rooms were on the first floor of the main building where Reverend Mother's office and sleeping quarters for the older nuns were also situated. Newly appointed to the Bordeaux residence, Reverend Mother had previously been the superior in Montpellier. In the short time since she had arrived at Nazareth House, many improvements had been made. Having obtained funding from the Ministry, the old, dilapidated buildings were renovated, and new clothes bought for the children. The food was healthy and plentiful and always well balanced, with fruit, vegetables and either chicken, fish or beef, with desserts of ice cream or cake relished with squeals of delight. On Sundays or school days off, we were able to take the group out to the park or for a walk into the city centre. When an Irish naval ship was docked in the harbour, we went to see it and were allowed on board to visit the deck. When Monsieur Chaban-Delmas was Mayor of Bordeaux, his wife organised a fête in the square for all the children of the city. We queued up with hundreds of family groups for the goody bags that she handed out to each child. Yells of joy were heard all around when they discovered coloured pencils, balloons and sweet treats in their bag. These were things that they rarely had and would keep in their bedside lockers or would use for swapping and bartering.

Social workers from the Dept. of Justice visited often. We usually met these on the premises to discuss each child's welfare and progress. We noted their good or bad behaviour and how each child was getting on. During these discussions, I reported anything I thought was relevant or important, but I felt totally inadequate as I realised early on that I lacked formal training and had no knowledge of the psychological jargon that was being used. I read up as much as I could on child psychology from the limited supply of reading material available.

Another Irish Sister and I had lessons in French once a week. These were very boring. We sat on either side of an old Redemptorist priest, who came in to teach us to read and write in French. He kept his eyes closed throughout the lesson. We fought back our laughter and made funny faces. As his gravelly voice droned on and on, we struggled to stay awake, but I did, however, learn to use the past participle and the future tense of the most useful verbs. During that first summer in Bordeaux, we were both sent on a training course to qualify as summer camp monitors. This entailed total immersion – staying at a college for one week. Most of the time, we attended workshops with discussions on the running of summer camps. This knowledge would later enable us to organise and participate in the holiday program during school holidays. We were the only nuns on the course and enjoyed ourselves immensely each night, meeting with the rest of the students at a sing-song sitting around a bonfire.

At no time during this period of my life did I question my vocation. I thanked God each day for having been called to this life, and although my vows were temporary and must be renewed each year, I was happy and committed to the Congregation. I enjoyed the work and prayer in an atmosphere of ongoing learning and enrichment. Early morning meditation, the recitation of the Divine Office and Mass were rigorously adhered to, and meals and recreation together with the rest of the Sisters were pleasant and enjoyable. Occasionally we had the distraction of a concert or pageant performed by the children. It was in the children's assembly hall in Bordeaux that I first watched the screening of the movie filmed in the west of Ireland called *The Quiet Man* starring John Wayne and Maureen O'Hara, with Irish actor Barry Fitzgerald also starring. Feeling that it betrayed the Irish people as rough and rowdy, I did not enjoy it, especially as I was in a foreign country surrounded by people who would identify me as similar to the characters.

When school term ended, it was time for the children and sisters to head off south to our very own summer residence in the Basses-Pyrénées. An ancient chateau had been purchased by the Order to facilitate our yearly getaway to the hills. Off came the school uniforms, and on went the t-shirts and shorts. Bags were packed.

Château de Belzunce in the tiny village of Méharin was our destination. The four-hour journey from Bordeaux through the region of Landes was anticipated with great excitement. Driven by Moise in the minibus, we stopped along the way at the beautiful seaside resort of Biarritz for a picnic and a visit to the Rocher de la Vierge. The sun beamed down on us in our serge habits and veils, obliging us to keep to the shady side of the beach. Thoughts of a swim in the cool blue waters were dissipated with a great struggle. Memories of Balbriggan beach and harbour caused me to suffer swallowing difficulties. Continuing on to the tiny village of Méharin, passing through towns, we witnessed the traditions kept alive by the Basque people; pelotte being played, processions or parades honouring the Holy days of their patron Saints, flags and bunting displaying their patriotic desire to be recognised as a separate entity from France. Sighting the church spire was the first indication that we were near our destination. Nestled in the hills and small mountains, the village seemed dwarfed by our castle looming on a height above the scattering of houses making up the landscape.

A group of Sisters and Adèle would have already been there a week before we arrived. Windows had been opened, rooms aired, and larders filled in readiness for our arrival. Prior to the Sisters purchasing the property, the old, dilapidated castle had been occupied by German forces during the last years of WWII. A somewhat valuable reminder of their presence had been left – in the form of timber panels dividing the large dormitories into single rooms where the sisters could sleep separately. The bedding was very basic, with dark ex-army blankets covering ancient iron bedsteads. The children were delighted with the freedom and carefree atmosphere. Whoops of joy rang out as they ran up and down the rickety stairs. An annexe building added on at a later date served as a refectory and playroom. Trainee educators provided plenty of games and artful activities indoors on rainy days. There were walking trips into the village, with the church being the venue for Mass and prayer for us nuns. The villagers were very religious. On Sunday afternoons, the sound of chanting Vespers could be heard for miles away. Monsieur le Curé wore a long, black, threadbare cassock and a filthy, greasy-looking biretta at all times. The Basque language was impossible to understand. Communication was limited, as not many villagers spoke French or English.

Without television or radio, we improvised lots of entertainment and amusement by having concerts, fancy dress, contests and games. Except for the landline telephone in Reverend Mother's bedroom, we were as far away from civilization as if we were stranded on a desert island. Most of all we loved our trips into the mountains, camping for days and exploring the countryside. Fortunately, only the older children were allowed to go as these trips leading into unknown, isolated terrain required stamina and strong legs. Such expeditions did, however, enable us to improve our survival skills, increase the children's sense of belonging and working within a team. Equipped with only the basics of one hairy army blanket each, a toothbrush, and a tin mug, the group was led by one of us Sisters, along with a student helper. We took with us a small saucepan, some matches and spoons together with a torch and some plasters. Other than that, we never planned ahead or really knew where the road would take us. When we got tired or hungry, we stopped and looked for someplace to camp. Not having tents, we sought out the owner of the nearest farmhouse to ask permission to sleep in his barn or outhouse. The local farmers were used to these visits. Welcoming us, they generously supplied us with fresh eggs, milk or an abundance of their surplus fruit and vegetables. Very often, we took up residence for the night in the upper storey of a cow byre where the hay would be stored to be lowered down through a trapdoor to the cattle below. In the morning, we'd cook our eggs and make our cocoa on a campfire. After a wash in the nearby stream, we'd be on our merry way again. Sometimes we found a bergerie. These were small stone-built huts dotted here and there in the mountains built by shepherds so they could take shelter at night. When the floor, consisting of dry earth covered with sheep droppings, was dusty and smelly, the children made witches' brooms with twigs to sweep it clean and gathered long grass and dry ferns to make beds to sleep on. The worst part of these escapades were the thunder and lightning storms that occurred regularly in the Basses-Pyrénées. These were frightening for me, especially when not accompanied by rain.

The nearest town from Méharin with a police station or a hospital was Saint-Palais. Being 12km away, we rarely reached there on foot.

Shopping was non-existent. But on one of our expeditions, we reached the tiny French-Spanish border town of Valcarlos. One side of the road was Spanish territory, but we were standing on the French side. We were able to purchase some nice Spanish chorizo and salami to eat with some French baguettes. Usually returning to Méharin after two or three days in the wild, a shower and a bed were most welcome.

At the end of the summer holidays, it was back to Bordeaux. Life continued through the children's schooldays. Work for us Sisters was not too difficult. Caring for the children, our commitments to religious life and changes in the seasons kept us busy, happy and content.

Hearing that President JF Kennedy had been shot on November 22 1963, I remember where I was standing. A student on work placement met me in the corridor saying that President Kennedy had been assassinated. In her last letter, my mother had mentioned the great welcome that he had received on his visit to Ireland a short time previously. The fact that she had mentioned it made it all the more poignant. As we did not have much news of what was happening on the world stage, this major news item triggered a bout of nostalgia and melancholy. I got over it as best I could.

On another occasion, I felt really upset and angry when a letter from home informing me of the death of my paternal grandmother was withheld from me for several weeks because it arrived during the season of Lent. Reading the letter on Easter Sunday, I was distraught by not having been at her funeral, and not at least being able to write to my father on the death of his mother. Memories of Granny Byrne flooded my brain. I thought of Aunts Isla and Annie, who lived with her in Church Road, of my father and his brothers and other sisters who would be grief-stricken. Born Ellen Nugent, Granny Byrne was a true matriarch, presiding over her family since the death of her husband, Nicolas. Visits to see her were always preceded by instructions to be on our best behaviour, to speak when spoken to and to not forget our manners. She was a much-loved mother and grandmother, kind, wise and a real legend. When one of the Sisters remarked on my subdued demeanour at recreation that day, Mother Superior casually mentioned that my grandmother had died. Darning a sock, with my head still bowed, I glanced over my glasses to see her grinning in a heartless way. Choking back tears, I remained silent until I was alone to cry and weep for the loss of such an important member of my family. I tried to shake off a growing feeling that I would love to see Balbriggan again. It was not just my family and friends who I longed to see. In my mind's eye, I imagined Drogheda Street, the neighbours, a daily swim at the black rock bathing place, going on the bus or train to Dublin city. It was hard to chase these images from my mind, but I soldiered on. I was enjoying the work with the children and kept busy. The routine helped me to pass the time, and I enjoyed the respite found during the hours passed in prayer and contemplation.

In the summer of 1965, my sister May married a lovely young man from County Leitrim. It was the second family wedding that I had not been able to attend, but I did not mind too much as they too would visit me in Bordeaux during their honeymoon in France. I was delighted to see them and to make acquaintances with my new brother-in-law, Pat McKeon. I was given permission to spend the day with them at Cap Ferret and Dune du Pilat, where we climbed the highest sand dune in Europe.

We made a day trip journey to Lourdes by train, during which we had the best laugh ever: Tall, dark and handsome, Pat cut a dashing figure. Our fellow lady passengers in the small carriage, eyeing him with curiosity, began to discuss his nationality. I translated to May and

Pat every word that they spoke between themselves in French. They argued that he looked Spanish and that he had handsome Latin looks. One of them contradicted this theory saying that his English accent was so good he could not possibly be Spanish or Italian. They had no idea that their conversation was being translated to the object of their admiration because they didn't know that I could understand every word. We laughed the whole time until we reached Lourdes and often recalled the episode many years later.

Their visit was a happy break from religious life. It buoyed me up and provided much-appreciated news from home and a certain amount of contact with the realities of life on the outside of the cocoon in which I was entombed. I was able to say goodbye and carry on in the life of prayer and work, believing in God's love, and that it all would be rewarded in the next life. None of the other Sisters ever had visits from their families. I never saw any visitors or family visiting the nuns living at Rue St Genès in Bordeaux. This may have been due to the fact that some of the French members of the community had been recruited from the ranks of young girls who had been protégés in the various Houses of the Congregation. Reared by the Sisters, they perhaps just progressed into religious life.

What happened next was a turning point for me. I wasn't aware that suddenly my world would come tumbling down. My beliefs were soon to be tested. I would soon be thrown off course. Fear, anxiety and horror were some of the emotions that were to shatter my very existence.

Chapter 24

THE BOMBSHELL

EARLY ONE MORNING, IN THE autumn of 1965, I was called to Reverend Mother's office and politely informed that I was being transferred to the Roquette prison in Paris. No reason was given. Nor did I expect any explanation. I received the news stoically, without showing any feelings or emotions. I accepted it obediently as I had been conditioned to do. It should not have come as any surprise. Detachment from people and places was constantly brought to mind during retreats and lectures. I was to proceed to my room to gather my belongings. I would be taking the midday train from Bordeaux to Paris the same day. There would be no time for goodbyes. I would simply vanish from where I had spent the past five years. It would be as if I had never existed. My name would probably never be mentioned again. At this point, I could not help feeling overwhelmed at the idea of returning to the prison. Life in Bordeaux with the children was in stark contrast to the life within the grim, dark walls of La Roquette. The work with women in prison was totally different from working with children. I left Bordeaux with a very heavy heart. On the train journey to Paris, I tried not to feel any sadness, but my emotions were all over the place. Was I being asked to do this penance for having been too happy?

How was I going to readjust to life in prison, working and dealing with adults? These questions and many more swam around in my head. The short period that I had previously spent at the prison had equipped me with very little experience.

It was dark when I arrived at La Roquette. Tiredness and hunger hung over me. Everything seemed black: the outer walls were stained by acid rain, the cinder track leading to the community pavilion showed not even a green weed protruding from the darkness underfoot. As I had spent some time here previously, I knew what it was going to be like. During the years in Bordeaux among the children, the work had been so interesting. I had acquired certain coping skills, which would not serve any purpose here. More fluent in the language now, and therefore understanding the swearing and obscenities coming from the detainees, I realised that I had absolutely no training or professional competence to deal with the situations that were arising. The sole purpose of my presence would be that of a surveillant.

The biggest obstacle confronting me was the sense of isolation. I was surrounded by people who I could not confide in. I could not speak of my feelings of depression to anyone: neither the detainees nor my associate Sisters. If I spoke of my difficulties to Mother Superior, it would sound like I was complaining. It was a constant struggle to eat or sleep. Food became tasteless and stuck in my throat. I lay awake for hours, trying to hold on to my sanity.

During this very trying time, I had a surprise visit from my cousin Micheál. He was studying astronomy and physics at University College Dublin. Travelling to Pic du Midi Observatory as part of his studies, he was accompanied by another student who was called De Valera. The fact that he was the President of Ireland's grandson filled me with a sense of nostalgic patriotism. They must have noticed how hard it was for me not to burst into tears when memories of Micheál's mother and father came flooding into my brain. Visions of the welcome that awaited everybody who visited them in their little cottage off Amiens Street in the northside of Dublin city flashed before me. I suddenly remembered Micheál taking me for the first time to the cinema in Dublin to see *Reach for The Sky* with Kenneth More playing the part of Douglas Badar, the true story of the airman who lost both his legs in WWII.

When asked how I was, I just blurted out that I was not happy. I didn't actually feel that I wanted to go home to Ireland because I had no notion of how that would be possible. Even if I did know, it would not make any difference. I was trapped without an escape route. There was no one I could talk to about how I felt. My state of mind was starting to show. I was tired. I tried to continue, but everything became an effort. I made mistakes, became forgetful and missed appointments. Confused about times and regulations, I was often late arriving for meals or to the chapel. I became an introvert. As weeks and months passed, these symptoms must have been noticed by my superior, for without discussion, I was sent to the Motherhouse in Le Dorat for a retreat. A rigorous round of sermons, prayer, meditations and strict silence did little to revive my enthusiasm. At no time did I have occasion to speak on a one-to-one basis with anyone who could help me physically or mentally. The retreat lasted two weeks, after which Mother Superior General summoned me to inform me that I was going back to Bordeaux. I understood from her tone that it would be expected of me to improve my attitude and mend my behaviour. This reprimand was likely to be the result of my lack of communication. I was becoming more and more non-verbal.

Chapter 25

MORE TRIALS AND TRIBULATIONS

EVEN THOUGH I WAS BACK in Bordeaux, there was no improvement in my situation. The light had gone out of my very existence. Without being consciously aware of my condition, I was suffering from homesickness, depression and despair. The Sisters welcomed me back, and the younger ones were kind in a friendly sort of way. Reverend Mother informed me that she had made an appointment for me to see a doctor. Off I went with her accompanying me. When we arrived at a building that looked like a monastery, I was ushered into a room where I was met by a monk dressed from chin to the ground in a long brown serge habit, tied around the waist with a thick white rope. Middle-aged, with a tanned complexion, he stared at me without speaking for what felt like ages. He ran his fingers through his slicked-back dark hair. Sitting opposite each other with a great mahogany desk separating us, his piercing eyes watched me for some time. I was dumbstruck. He then began to question me about my appetite and whether I was sleeping, but I couldn't answer. Any words escaping my lips made little sense. Totally flabbergasted, I remember feeling resentment towards this person. Not having chosen to see him, I felt I was being judged, after which a report would be given to Reverend Mother, of which I would

Away… for God's Sake

never know the contents. I found his glaring face quite intimidating; I did not think that I could confide in him or that he was trustworthy. I had no intention of speaking to him. My anger and resentment must have become apparent. His tone and choice of words meant little to me. His demeanour stifled any effort to communicate. The interview did not last long, and no other appointment was arranged.

A few days later, Reverend Mother handed me a bottle of pills without any label. She told me the doctor had prescribed them, adding that Doctor Matignon, who I had seen, was a psychiatrist. This information was annoying. Paranoia was starting to play havoc on my mind. I felt that I was being persecuted by this overpowering woman. Nonetheless, I continued to pray and work as best I could. Needless to say, I never took the tablets.

A young English Sister, who I had known in the Novitiate, and I were seated in the children's playground when out of the blue, she told me that she would love to see her father. She explained that when her mother had died, her Irish father, living in London, had sent her into the care of his sister. This aunt was a Sister in Baldock and she convinced her to join the Congregation. I asked her if she had told Mother Superior of her longing to see her father.

"No," she replied, "I'm just going to write to him asking him to send me the money for my fare back to England. I've got a few things ready for my departure, and when I have my fare, I'll just walk out." She then ran up to her room to fetch the "few things" and showed me a blue satin toilet bag. I couldn't help laughing when she opened it. Inside the bag were five or six hair rollers, a hairbrush and a few hair clips.

"When I went to Lourdes, Mother Superior gave me some cash to buy holy medals and a picture of the Virgin Mary to send to my Dad, but I bought these instead," she confided to me.

This conversation made me think that maybe I should say something soon to the Superior about my longing to see my family. A few months later, in her office, when questioned about my state of mind, I mentioned that I was tired, that I felt depressed. The conversation turned to Ireland, and thinking of home just made me burst into tears. I knew that two of the Irish novices with whom I had been in the Novitiate had been allowed home for a holiday before their final vows. Trying to communicate with a person in authority, whilst in a very emotional state, was not easy. Expressing the desire for a visit home, saying that it might settle me in preparation for final vows, I choked out words to that effect. It was the middle of November 1966, and there were still seven months left before I would have to make final vows, after which I would be allowed a vacation. She reddened in disbelief at my sheer audacity. I left her office, wondering if I had approached things the proper way. I had been dismissed and rebuked. There was nothing further discussed, and off I went back to my work.

Chapter 26

DEFROCKING

THE VERY NEXT AFTERNOON, SISTER Assistant called me into her office and led me to a small table where there were some sheets of paper and a pen. These documents were written in French. I remember thinking that this was a procedure whereby I could continue to remain in Bordeaux until my temporary vows would expire six months later and that at that time, my situation would be reviewed. This was evidently not the case. Reverend Mother's assistant placed her finger at the bottom where I was to sign my name. Zombie-like, I signed, not realising that it was a typed letter addressed to the Archbishop of Bordeaux requesting a dispensation of my temporary vows. The next page was a declaration to the effect that I would not have any claim for any future monetary recompense. I had the impression that this was some sort of routine procedure normally signed by everyone. I had no choice anyway because I was ordered to do so. While doing as I was told, signing these papers, I had no idea what was in store for me, and nobody enlightened me. I said nothing to anybody and continued on oblivious for the rest of the day.

When in bed that same night, just starting to doze off, a knock on my door deprived me of slumber. I opened the door to Sister Assistant's blank expression and frosty voice, telling me to go immediately to the parlour in the entrance building. The time was 10 pm. Half asleep, I followed her instructions. There, laid out on a chaise longue, was a coat, a tartan pleated skirt complete with a large pin, and a mustard-coloured, woollen twinset consisting of a jersey and a cardigan, a pair of yellow laced suede shoes and the inevitable headscarf. I was to dress quickly as there was a taxi coming to take me to the railway station. To say I was in shock is putting it mildly. I had no idea that these clothes had been purchased already, and here I was being sent like a fugitive into the cold and dark November night. Numb in mind and body, accompanied in the taxi by a silent and impervious Mother Superior, I was surprised when she boarded the train also. I sat beside her so as not to have to see her stony face.

Halfway through the journey, she offered me a sandwich, which I ate, not knowing when I would see food again. Prayer, or any kind of communication with the Almighty, was far from my mind. As far as I was concerned, He had abandoned me long before I had shed the outward trappings of religious life. Sister de Lorette no longer existed. I was being cast out in the darkness of night like a fugitive, a leper, without a word of farewell. Gazing down at my feet for most of that train journey, the shoes I was wearing reminded me that from now on, my life would be different. I was going home unaware if my family had been informed of my pending arrival. It never crossed my mind to envisage what their reaction would be. Fear or anticipation of the future did not occur to me. Drifting in and out of sleep, reality and dreams intermingling, the sound of the moving train was my only comfort as I sat upright in that darkened carriage. Had I really made this journey in reverse all those years ago as a confident, healthy seventeen-year-old? Here I was now – a trembling wreck, a distant relative of that young girl, wearing clothes hanging on a skeletal frame and resembling a clothes hanger. When we reached Orly Airport, I was tired and distraught, but a little joy crept into my heart at the thought of going home after so many years. Much to my discomfort, Mother Superior boarded the plane to Dublin. I had not uttered one word to her, and she did not address me even once. At some time during the flight, she opened her bag and handed me an envelope, informing me that it contained something to tide me over. It contained the princely sum of 35 Irish pounds, which I handed to my mother as soon as I arrived in Drogheda Street. I never did discover what reason or explanation Mother Superior gave my parents for my sudden repatriation, but I got the impression that I was being dumped and that the Order was glad to have gotten rid of a problem.

Part 3

Chapter 27

HOME

THE PLANE SHOOK VIOLENTLY. THE turbulence continued for far too long. Rain battered the small windows. Holding onto the armrests, fearing that I would not reach Dublin airport, I also felt happy and excited in anticipation of seeing my family and country again. Torrential rain and wind continued to beat against us as we touched down. Emerging onto the steps leading to the flooded Irish soil, my heart skipped a beat. It was eight and a half long years since I last stood on home ground. It was one of the happiest moments of my life. A wave of joy buoyed me up as I walked in the rain to the terminal building, where my parents were waiting for me. They did not look in my direction at first. Instead, their eyes, in shock and horror mixed with awe, gazed at the person accompanying me. They obviously had no idea that she would be with me. They were still in shock when they greeted me without showing either joy or sorrow. I supposed that all that was going through their heads was how they were going to deal with this unexpected guest. Heavy rain and gale-force winds continued as we made our way to the car park. I deduced that their mode of transport was to blame for their embarrassment and anguish and not the fact that I had arrived home. My father's old Raleigh bicycle had been replaced by an automobile. The partly blocked out words LYONS TEA could be seen under a splash of grey paint on the side of my father's ancient Ford transit van. When the passenger side door slid open to reveal an old airplane seat that was not attached to the floor, my mother and I climbed into the back to sit on a spare wheel and another loose airplane seat. Mother Superior got into this front seat and held on for dear life to a leather strap on the roof, while my father, puffing, panting and coughing, struggled with the ignition. Soon we were in Balbriggan. Oh! The sheer joy of seeing Drogheda Street. I was exhilarated to be home again. It was late afternoon, and the fire was lit in the front room. The china teacups were brought out of the china cabinet, and homemade bread was served on small plates. This was all for the benefit of "her Reverence".

After going to splash some water on my face, I entered the kitchen/ living room. I was amazed to see three men sitting at the dinner table with my father. One of them I recognised as my eldest brother Nicky. The other two were seated with their backs to me, looking at a TV perched on a fridge. They were engrossed in watching a cartoon, which I later learned was the Flintstones. The two strangers turned simultaneously. "Howaya, Our" were their first words. This was like music to my ears as I came face to face with my two younger brothers Malachy and Thomas, now grown young men. The little boys I had left behind were now in their twenties, gravel-voiced and sporting stubbly chins. The term 'Our' is the manner in which clans in Balbriggan refer to family members. I felt that I had really and truly arrived among my own people. I was accepted as if I had never been away.

A lot had changed in the house in my absence: the old range had been replaced by a beige and brown tile surround fireplace; the high mantelpiece was gone; a small fridge in the corner had replaced the ancient meat safe previously nailed outside on the garden wall. But most surprising of all was that the large, old, now-silent Pye wireless on the windowsill had been replaced by a black and white television. A new electric cooker now stood where the old gas cooker used to be. There was now a twin tub washing machine in the scullery, complete with a wringer, which was called a mangle. My mother was delighted to demonstrate how this worked – by feeding the wet clothes through two rubber rollers while turning a handle. A brass electric kettle nestled on the windowsill in the kitchen. The sewer outside the back no longer smelled of Jeyes Fluid. This had been replaced by the more sophisticated aroma of Dettol.

My baby sister Claire had grown into a 15-year-old teenager with beautiful, natural blonde hair. A pupil of Loreto Secondary School, she had developed quite a personality and chatted about her studies and her friends. Frances had morphed into a fabulous young woman of many talents and skills. Employed in Hair Fashions in Harcourt Street Dublin, she was unrecognisable except for her vaguely familiar face. Seeing her again on that first day, my younger sister no longer looked like the child I remembered. She was standing with her back to the fireplace. Her blond ringlets, replaced by a back-combed bouffant hairstyle gently flicked out at the ends, framed a beautiful smiling face. Dressed in a beige cashmere polo necked sweater, a short tweed skirt and knee-high suede leather boots, she looked so much like a grown-up lady. Whatever she was thinking at seeing me, she kept to herself. However, she proceeded there and then to wash and blow-dry my short, spiked hair! Hours later, lying together in the small bed we shared in the upstairs back room, I gazed in wonder at her many outfits hanging on the clothes rail behind the door. Handbags, leather footwear, and hats filled the only shelf in the room. When she showed me pictures of Mary Quant's fashion designs and model Twiggy, I became bewildered at this whole new world opening out in front of me. Gone were the below-the-knee pleated dresses and gathered dirndl skirts. These were replaced by skimpy miniskirts worn by teenagers and young women. Quant had taken the fashion world by storm, making her latest designs available in High Street stores at affordable prices. Photos of Frances's recent holiday in Palma, Majorca showed her sunbathing with her workmates, surrounded by tanned admiring lotharios. Filled with both excitement and panic, I wondered how and where I would fit into this strange environment that I had suddenly landed into. Many years later, she told me that the worst part of my appearance was the outdated plaid skirt with the pin. The skirt was for someone twice my size and reached nearly to the ground.

May was now living in Limerick with her husband, Pat. I would see them the following day. Helen was on hand to entertain Mother Superior and, much to the relief of my parents, took her to stay overnight in her home in Skerries. I had no desire to bid her farewell and do not recall her last words to me. Sometime after her departure, I noticed my sister Claire had a toilet bag. It looked vaguely familiar. I asked where she had got it, and she told me Mother Superior had given it to her. Well, well, I recognised it as the same bag that Sister Alice had shown me. I knew for certain then that she had been repatriated to London and that the bag had been confiscated or she had left it behind in her hurried exit from the convent in Bordeaux.

The clothes I wore on that first day home were the only things I possessed. I had no change of underwear, toiletries or haircare. I did not know much about currency or the cost of living. Having no idea of how I would reintegrate into everyday life in a small town, I felt forlorn and alien. These feelings of desolation and isolation were soon dispatched by the warmth and generosity of my family. Intermittent moments of joy and exuberance began replacing my insecurity and thoughts of failure and inadequacy.

I did not feel like praying or discussing religion. While my parents and siblings had retained the faith and practice acquired in the past, I found these beliefs no longer applied to me. Childhood nurturing in that respect had somehow been shaken and lost while in France. Disillusionment and dislike for all things pertaining to the parochial scene meant that nothing made sense to me and were no more than rituals. In other words, my soul was empty and troubled. Enjoyment in the liturgy was gone and had been replaced with disappointment and bitterness. I envied my peers their utter steadfast faith in God and the Church. While in France, I had never participated in parish activities, so taking part in church services felt strange. I no longer felt included. Without a sense of belonging, I was now an outsider looking in through a clouded window. Struggling spiritually, I tried to shed the skin and feathers of my previous existence in religion. No longer having to observe rules, regulations or rituals, it took quite a while for a slow recovery from guilt. This crept in gradually, until the heaviness of the black cloud was lifted from my mind. A glimmer of inner peace increased as the days and months passed. I began to laugh and enjoy the company of other people again. Free from routine, each day brought unexpected joy and happiness.

To add to this happiness at being home, there was an addition to the family. A dog named Boots had come into our family some years previously. A Highland terrier, he was the most lovable and friendly dog. I instantly fell in love with him. Not having had any contact with animals or pets for so many years, I was thrilled to take him for walks and to run with him on the beach. To see the Martello tower, the old

Bathhouse and the diving board where I had spent my childhood gave me a new lease of life. The gentle sound of the waves lapping on the sand, shingle and stones was a source of great delight.

When the tide had ebbed, I ran with Boots to the Sailor's Grave beyond the cliffs. Throwing a large stone on the mound in memory of those poor sailors who lost their lives when their ship the Bell Hill had been washed up on the rocks on 26th February 1875, uttering a prayer for all those who had been lost at sea throughout the world, I smiled thinking about the reason Balbriggan people are sometimes referred to as 'Balbriggan Half Shirts'. When the cargo of the Bell Hill was washed up, rolls of material were salvaged and made into short shirts by the locals. In revenge for this moniker, Balbriggan people called the inhabitants of nearby Skerries the "Skerries Goats" because legend relates that St. Patrick's goat had been killed and eaten by the natives when the Saint landed on one of the small islands near Skerries.

Sometimes I felt as if I had never been away. Every now and again, I was able to forget the years I had spent away in France. During that first winter home, the sounds and sights of the high tides lashing against the lighthouse and crashing over the harbour wall were a source of intense pleasure. The smells and tastes of my mother's cooking were another great boost to my health and wellbeing. Enjoying meals with my family, I quickly gained a few pounds in weight and began less and less to resemble a scarecrow.

At no time was I asked why I had not stayed away. I suppose it was obvious to all that I had been homesick and unhappy. I was never made to feel inadequate or a failure. There were no questions asked as to what I intended to do now with my life, but one thing was uppermost in my mind: I would have to start earning my living.

It was usual practice to work and earn wages, pay for one's board and lodgings while living in the family home, and contribute to the household expenses. All young people working and living at home were expected to hand up a portion of their wages. The rest of the money paid for fares, clothes and entertainment, or was saved. So off I went to the Social Security office in Station Street to obtain a number, which I would have to present to any prospective employer. Bernadette O'Rourke greeted me with a smile, and in a friendly manner, informed me that my old P.P.S number was still on record from when I worked in Smyth's factory. My employment prospects were drastically poor. Lacking in self-confidence, I had no notion of where I would start to look for work. Not having had an employer for so many years, I had no references. Even though I had experience working with children with behavioural problems, there didn't appear to be any openings in this area of employment. With no formal qualification in teaching or the French language, teaching would be impossible to get into. Being bilingual equated to nothing if I had no commercial or business experience. The future looked bleak.

Starting to work in the local hotel as a waitress was easy. Lots of weddings and dress dances meant I was kept busy. A chance meeting with Miss McDonald, my past favourite teacher, encouraged me to take a refresher course at night to upgrade my book-keeping skills.

The arrival of May and Pat's first child in May 1967 was a source of great joy and excitement. I became an aunty. A beautiful first grandchild for my parents, the little girl was named Gráinne. She sat in her pram and bounced up and down whenever the music from Z Cars was played on TV. We were delighted when the McKeon family moved back to live in Balbriggan. With all the things happening in my life now, there was never a dull moment or time for me to dwell on what might have been if I had remained away. Day to day life was becoming bearable, and I felt secure back in the family home.

My father was working in his workshop in Church Street. Back in 1964, when Miss Warren, the owner of the premises and property called Laragh, had decided to sell her entire estate, she offered my father the first option to purchase. Her estate consisted of a three-story manor, a one-acre orchard garden, together with outhouses, a cobbled courtyard and a dilapidated coach house. The property occupied the corner of Hampton Street and Church Street and could be entered by a large gate in either street. This offer was a major dilemma for my parents. Faced with the prospect of eviction and the loss of his business or having to borrow heavily, they decided on the latter. My father was able to secure a loan from Property, Loan and Investment Company in Dublin in order to buy the property. For the sum of 850 pounds, he became the proud owner of his domain. As the quarterly repayments amounted to a lot more than the rent that he had been paying the landlady, these payments were a constant source of struggle and stress for many years to come. He trained quite a few apprentices to be carpenters.

Many years later, my brother and I visited one such graduate in Moneymore, County Sligo, called Frank O'Connor. He related the story of the missing penny. While Frank was an apprentice with my father, Mr Taylor, who owned Ardgillan Castle, approached my father to ask if he could fix one of the many gates leading up to the castle. Frank accompanied his boss to the gate. With his usual ingenuity, my father proceeded to balance one side of the gate with the help of a big new penny wedged between the pintle and gudgeon. With the problem solved, off they went. Sometime later, Mr Taylor repeated his request, and the men returned to see that the gate was again not opening and swinging properly. On inspection, it was discovered that the penny was missing. After it was replaced, and stolen again, Frank and one of his mates decided to keep a watch at the scene of the crime. On a dark and cold evening, peeping out from behind bushes, they spied and identified the culprit taking the penny. Nicknamed "The Gulf", the poor unfortunate nearly fainted when Frank and company jumped out of their hiding place. At that time, a penny could be used in the gas meter that most houses had under the stairs. Piped gas was supplied from the local gas works, which were situated between Mill Street and Quay Street. The River Bracken separated the huge gas tank from Cumisky's coal yard. Our gas meter was under the stairs in what we called the coal hole. When Mr Connelly came to empty this meter, we sat around our kitchen table watching him make stacks of 12 pennies amounting each to one shilling. Sometimes there was a surplus when the amount surpassed the meter reading. This surplus was deemed a rebate and was distributed to us by my mother.

Nicky was working in my father's workshop. Malachy and Thomas were employed locally and had many friends calling to the house after football matches. They enthralled us with stories of their escapades and trips to Ballybunion. It was around this time my father got involved with terrier racing. He enjoyed going to the dog trials and had a few winners. My mother was a member of the Irish Country Women's Association and had joined a choir conducted by Fr. Griffin. It was lovely to see her getting all dolled up in her choral attire whenever the choir travelled to perform.

It was wonderful to be home on that first Christmas. On Christmas Eve, my mother and my brother Nicky took me to the pub for a drink. Mary Jane Hall's grocery shop and bar in Bridge Street was the venue. We entered by the front door of the house, took two steps down into a snug and were served through a hatch from the shop. I remember tasting the Babycham that was offered to me and enjoying being a part of regular society in a grown-up way. Having missed out on my teenage years and early twenties, I had no idea of what films, magazines or music were in vogue. Clothes were not a problem. The one set of garments I stood up in on my arrival being all I possessed, I was grateful to my sisters who supplemented my apparel with gifts of sweaters and raincoats during that first winter.

The lay training assistant whom I had worked with in Bordeaux was now corresponding with me. Marie France Taillandier, now living in Le Mans, was in her early twenties. I invited her to come on holiday to Ireland. Meeting at the airport, we had an awesome reunion. She was delighted to see that I was looking well and happy being back with my family. It was great to freshen up on my French while reminiscing about our time in Bordeaux. Before her departure, she looked at me and remarked seriously that I should now consider moving out of my parents' house and lead a more independent lifestyle. Neither agreeing nor disagreeing, I didn't give the idea much thought, but it would not be much later when the occasion to leave home again would present itself. Marie France kept in touch, and she got married soon after to Gerard Poirier. Our friendship was of a lasting nature and proved to be to our mutual advantage for many years to come.

However, the novelty of being home in Balbriggan was often replaced by anxiety. Adjusting to life back in Balbriggan consisted of an enormous uphill journey. I knew absolutely nothing about finances or making decisions about money. Cheques, money orders, and savings accounts sounded like a foreign language. Even the cost of a postage stamp eluded me. Food, that precious commodity that I had taken for granted, had to be purchased and paid for. It needed to be stored, cooked and presented, portioned, and leftovers used up. The hairdressing salon was a totally new experience. I had to find a doctor's surgery and a dentist. The chemist shop was a wonderland of health and beauty lotions and potions. I had never voted in an election. All of these everyday, normal activities demanded decisions I had never had to make in convent life. Being able to gather together some personal possessions that would belong to me exclusively gave my morale a tremendous boost. Visiting the local library and choosing what I wanted to read was a special occasion.

The weeks following my return were a mixture of stress and excitement. My mother was a great mentor. She helped me enormously to slip gently back into family life, even though my exit from religious life must have been a disappointment for her. If it was, she never made me feel that I had failed in some way. The years I spent away from home were never mentioned. The smell of her brown bread and buttered scones brought a heavenly scent to my nostrils. Soon I was putting some flesh back on my skeletal frame. Most of all, her smile would light up a room, and her wise words encouraged me to embrace whatever challenges were thrown at me. I was amazed at other members of the family expressing their opinions as I listened in wonder when discussions arose around the family table. These discussions sometimes ended in arguments, but it was so interesting to listen to my family talk about politics, current affairs, crime, accidents and tragedies. Open debate was something that had been missing during my cloistered past.

I continually endeavoured to integrate myself into life in the local community. Balbriggan was still a small industrial town. Smyths and Stevenson factories were still manufacturing clothing and hosiery. Hampton Mills on Market Green employed many people, and Wavin

Pipes had been established on Dublin Road in 1962 by a Dutch company.

Shopping trips by train to Dublin city were frequent. I marvelled at the sight of Ardgillan Castle as the train passed under the Lady's Stairs at Barnegeera. At each stop, I relived my childhood excitement watching the people getting on and off the train, realising that no one was staring at me in the way people did when I was dressed in long black habit and veil. I was now just ordinary and unnoticed. When the train crossed the rail bridge before coming into Malahide, and I could see the sea on both sides, it was heaven to my eyes. I was seeing familiar landmarks with newfound enthusiasm. Arriving at Amiens Street Railway Station brought back great memories. I felt a great shock and a sense of loss at seeing that the place where the famous landmark, Nelson's Pillar, had been in the middle of O'Connell Street, was now an empty space. Blown up in March 1966 by the IRA in an effort to rid the city of reminders of British Imperialism, its loss invoked a sense of nostalgia. Together with Clerys big clock, which was still there, Nelson's Pillar had been the favourite rendezvous for friends and lovers for generations of Dubliners. Another huge building had appeared in Eden Quay in my absence. Opened in 1965, Liberty hall at that time became the tallest building in Dublin. But it never became as much a favourite rendezvous as Nelson's Pillar.

Chapter 28

THE NIGHTMARES

My PEACE OF MIND WAS, however, shattered one morning just before Christmas by a letter dated 18th December, which arrived from the Motherhouse in Le Dorat. Attached to a letter written by Mother Jérôme, the assistant Mother General of the Congregation, was a letter from the Archbishop of Bordeaux dispensing me from my vows. Addressing me as "Ma pauvre enfant," the tone of Mother Jérôme's message insinuated that I was a lost soul and that my conscience would forever haunt me. This reprimand took me back to a state of depression, which I attempted to shrug off. It was around that time that the nightmares began.

Going through a dark place, suddenly the walls would begin closing in, with the ceiling starting to fall on top of me. A blood-curdling scream would wake me up before the ceiling or walls landed. The high-pitched shriek would also awaken the whole household. With my heart pounding and throbbing, and breathing with difficulty, I would struggle to get to the window or door of the bedroom. My mother came each time to help me back to bed. Everyone in the house would be awake by now. The neighbours' lights would go on to see if there was anyone being murdered in the street. Soon everyone got used to the regular screaming and would just turn over and go back to sleep. For me, however, it was and still is to this day a regular occurrence. I experience the same nightmare of being smothered by falling roofs or walls collapsing, trapping me underneath. It can sometimes be a tunnel where I am nearly at the end, but before I can escape, an iron grille slams down in front of me. Relief comes when I wake up suddenly to realise it has only been a nightmare. Such occasions cause me to be very tired the following day, especially whenever I am unable to sleep for the remainder of the night.

Even though I was adjusting well to life back in Ireland, there were some areas of my life I avoided dealing with. My relationship with spirituality was still stagnant. There was no solution to my lack of faith. All my thoughts were of a practical nature. With encouragement from family, I sought help, and my GP recommended counselling. I talked through my dilemma many times with professionals, but this was of no avail. It was obvious that I was suffering from post-traumatic stress disorder, especially at the start of my emergence back into living in the real world. The nightmares continued without me being consciously aware of the suppressed anguish causing them.

The absence of friends was another hurdle that had to be jumped. My childhood friends and school classmates had married or had moved away. With the remaining constraints of the rules of detachment still within me, how was I ever going to be able to form close relationships? Would I be able to confide in or trust another human being? What is a true friend? These questions, although subtle, existed, lingered and troubled my lonely waking moments.

Away… for God's Sake

Chapter 29

BALBRIGGAN MOTORS

FINDING A JOB WAS UPPERMOST on my agenda. With very few qualifications and a huge gap of unaccounted years, I was eager to obtain employment where I could use my French. Teaching was out because of my lack of a diploma or degree. With no evidence to show my knowledge of the language, I contacted the Alliance Francaise in Dublin and arranged an appointment. My mother came with me as I had no idea how to find my way around Dublin. I was soon able to sit for an exam and obtain the Diplôme de Langue Française with honours from the Ministère de l'Éducation Nationale, Paris, dated 5th July 1967. After many unsuccessful applications for employment, and prior to obtaining this qualification, I was able to get a job in the office of a local garage.

I had heard that there was a vacancy in the office of Balbriggan Motors. This garage in Station Street was a hive of activity owned by Mr Dan Macken. It employed two fully fledged mechanics plus a few apprentices. Mary Loughry was leaving her job in the office and informed me that if I was interested, I was to go to the premises and ask for a Mr John Carroll.

The huge doors were wide open as I entered. The sound of a

radio blaring together with the sound of hammering, loud voices, and the deafening shrill of the phone coming from the office created a deafening cacophony. Not seeing anybody resembling a suit and tie clad manager, I stumbled between gas cylinders, spare wheels, scattered toolboxes and addressed two feet and legs protruding out from under an ancient Model T Ford.

"I'm looking for Mr John Carroll," I shouted over the din. The legs grew longer. A body appeared wearing greasy overalls, lying on a flat piece of wood on wheels.

"That's me," was the reply from this apparition of a handsome young man in a boiler suit covered in grease, attempting to clean his hands with a filthy oily rag. He took a good look at me and informed me that Mary Loughry's Aunt Bridget would "show me the ropes," and if I was interested, the job was mine. Bookkeeping was the main task, and I soon found myself busy doing the invoices, posting these to the sales and purchases ledgers, and writing up the employees' daily jobs. Payments made by the customers were recorded, and receipts written out. The phone rang often, with clients wanting to know if their vehicle was ready. Mary Dunphy, the senior mechanic Paddy Dunphy's sister, would arrive each Thursday with a jam and cream sponge sandwich cake from Spicer's bakery for morning tea. This was divided among us, cut with a chisel in the absence of a knife. I loved every minute of the work as it was close to home, and the wage of five pounds a week was a godsend. Working in an all-male environment was a novelty and proved enlightening once I got to know the lingo. All types of people came and went into the office. Nicknames were very common. Acquainting myself with the characters bearing these monikers was both entertaining and interesting. The Dozer was a barber, and Hoppy had a limp. The Giant was very small. Coppertop sported a bald head. Steak was the local butcher, and Split the Wind a hackney driver. The Mull was a newspaper reporter and Joiner a carpenter. There was the Bilsh, Birdie, Blary, Boggy, Bonser, Budgie, Bully, Dargle, Didler, Gonny, Durango, Goggy, Gulf, Gub, Jap, Jazzer, Jinty, Jizzy, J.F., Midler, Miler, Neddy, Nodgy, Puddeners, Rowdy, The Ruck, Tubby, Tuffy, the Sheriff, Spider, Sniggy, Stuff her, Windy and Wiggy. These names were in no way derogatory. On the contrary, they elevated their owners to lovable, popular and much-loved characters, who were remembered as legends long after they had departed this life.

Ironically only one female was ever mentioned in the same breath as these well-known male icons. This was none other than The Janeo. Having a full-time job in Stevenson's factory, Jane Seaver was one of the best wallpaper hangers and painter decorators in her spare time.

This newfound independence allowed me to settle back into family life, but I was still very naive and raw socially. My sisters, particularly Frances, were a great help. Frances took me to dances in the Pavilion Ballroom in nearby Skerries. Oh, the joy of dancing again in Frances' borrowed green velvet dress (with her permission this time) with a hairdo and make-up helping my lack of confidence. Her friends welcomed me, and we enjoyed listening to the bands playing and being twirled round in the arms of any young man who chose to ask us to dance. When the music stopped, if a fellow asked for the next dance, then we hoped that would lead to a mineral at the bar. If this happened, an invitation to "leave you home" followed. Life was for living, and rediscovering the joy of even the smallest and most insignificant of life's pleasures was a great morale boost.

The closing years of the 1960s was a great time to be young and single. The social life was good, and many young people were enjoying the music mania started by the Beatles. Dance halls were bursting at weekends. Most people were smoking and drinking alcohol at these venues. Skiffle groups strummed a beat with brooms strung on tea chests and created rhythms on glass washboards. Rock 'n' roll, jiving and jitterbugging were taking over from the more traditional waltzes, tangos, foxtrots and quicksteps favoured by the older generation.

When John Carroll and I attended the wedding of one of his friends, we danced together a good deal during the evening reception. John was a great dancer and loved Buddy Holly, Chubby Checker and could jive and do the twist beautifully. Elvis Presley and Tom Jones tunes kept us on our feet throughout some crazy nights. It was indeed a great change for me. I had missed out on lots of mixing with young people during my adolescence and early twenties.

Traditional Irish live music was popular and began to be played in pubs around the country. This inspired publicans to modernise their lounges and to install ladies' toilets. Carpets, curtains and open fires were introduced, and the ladies flocked to places which were hitherto a male domain. I loved being part of this scene and frequented most of the pubs in Skerries and Balbriggan.

There was still part of my well-being that was being tested. Constantly struggling to reconcile harmoniously within the rituals and practice of my faith and religion, I was confused. My belief in religious practice was now somehow disrupted. I attended Sunday Mass as was expected, but it did nothing to dispel my distaste. I went for all the wrong reasons: as it was expected, I did not wish to rock the boat, to see who was there, what they were wearing, and to hear what was going on in the parish. Although Mass was no longer said in Latin, and with the altar now facing the congregation, it was very different to the small chapel of the convent, where there were no distractions of children crying or fancy hairstyles in front. My newfound freedom also played a big part in my gradual distancing from God and all spirituality. Neither berthed safely in the faith of my childhood nor firmly anchored in the Catholic Church, my soul was now cast adrift in an unknown ocean.

It wasn't long before I started seeing John outside of working hours. Invoices were written out to customers for repairs to their cars, tractors or trucks. Labour costs were priced by John and handwritten by me. Without a calculator or adding machine, this was a long, drawn-out process and required coming back occasionally to the office in the evening. John would have gone home and changed into his Sunday clothes, and his great crop of curly, black hair would be tamed down with a generous amount of Brylcreem. It was then customary to go to the pub for a drink. After a few such episodes, it was accepted that we were seeing each other outside of work. I was happy to have a boyfriend, and the fact that he was the boss was an added bonus. Meeting his mother for the first time made it somehow official. My parents were pleased that I was living a "normal" life and doing things like other people of my age, such as working, socialising and keeping up my appearance. His friends and relations became my friends. He gave me a beautiful gold bracelet at Christmas. We attended weddings together and enjoyed visits to the city with chicken and chips from the chipper after the pub. On one memorable occasion, we joined his sister Finn and her husband Jimmy Rock on a trip to Tralee and Killarney, where we trotted by pony and trap around the famous lakes.

During this time, a house phone had been installed at home. I was surprised one evening when my mother informed me that a French man had been trying to contact me and had left his Dublin telephone number. Mr Henri Borguet, having enquired at the Alliance Francaise for a suitable bilingual person to join his staff in Dublin, had my name passed on to him. We arranged to meet in a local hotel for an interview. He offered me the job as his personal secretary, with a salary of ten pounds per week. I accepted and started sometime later.

His import/export business consisted of importing marine engines and spare parts for fishing boats used by Irish fishing fleets all around the Irish coast. Price lists and other technical information needed to be translated, together with correspondence between Irish and French agents. Mr Borguet was also the Marine Attaché in Ireland, which meant that any French offshore trawler with a sick or injured crewman on board could contact his office for the necessary help. Organising an ambulance to be dispatched to meet the stricken patient and arranging subsequent hospitalisation was very satisfying work. I really enjoyed this interesting occupation, and using my language skills and improving my French vocabulary made me very happy indeed.

I travelled to work in Dublin in a car owned and driven by Joe McCormack, who was living over Landy's pub in Drogheda Street. Nuala Kenny was picked up on the Square and Mary Curran at Market Green corner. Mary and I chatted in the back seat, both going and returning home in the evening. We discussed helping a mother in High Street who had a daughter with Downs Syndrome. Knowing the mother well, we approached her offering to look after her daughter whenever she needed a break to go to the hairdresser or other appointments. She was delighted to accept. Word soon spread that we were interested in starting a minding service for other children with special needs on a voluntary basis. Parents with special needs children contacted us and got involved. We were offered the use of a classroom in the technical school in Skerries on Saturday mornings. Hughie Reilly, whose young son was being cared for at home by his parents, was the first to offer his services. He was available to drive to and from Skerries, together with any children who need to be taken along. Volunteers too numerous to mention helped out, especially Nick McGuinness and Jackie Hunt.

As there were absolutely no services available at the time for children with special needs, the parents, being the sole carers and educators, spent all day every day without a break. In a very short space of time, we were taking up to 15 to 20 children every Saturday morning. They came from Balbriggan, Rush, Lusk, Skerries and surrounding areas. The service was voluntary and free of charge. It was gratifying enough for us to see the smiling faces of parents as they left their children in. We offered biscuits and milk, played ring-a-ring-a-rosy and sang nursery rhymes. In fine weather, we played in the front yard. This, however, caused us to get a fright when one girl climbed on the low front wall. She could then be seen floating away slowly. Luckily, we were able to retrieve her from the back of the coal lorry she had jumped onto, which was slowly moving away.

Parents formed a committee in order to raise funds for the purchase of equipment. A sponsored walk was organised, and the necessary funds raised allowed us to buy furniture, toys and insurance. Everything was going well until one Saturday morning when two elderly ladies arrived asking us to provide evidence of our qualifications! They had not informed us who they were, but we learned afterwards that they were officials from some Government Department. Mary and I were soon superfluous to requirements, the children being taken into daily care by St Michael's House in Dublin. We were never recognised for our voluntary work nor our input into the foundation of the Fingal Association, which was later to become Prosper Fingal. This had been the nearest I came to actually using the childcare skills I had acquired in Bordeaux.

There was great excitement in our family in the summer of '68. Preparations were underway for my sister Frances' wedding to Brendan Keady. It would be the first time for me to be a bridesmaid. Having missed Helen's and May's weddings, I was thrilled to be part of this family celebration. Frances and Brendan were married in St Peter and Paul's Church in Balbriggan. It was an important occasion, reuniting both the Byrne and Hoey families and making acquaintance with the Keady family. Helen, Claire and I were Frances' bridesmaids. Our long pale green, high neck dresses with puffed sleeves were specially designed and made by a Dublin dressmaker. Frances always looked like a film star, but on that day, she dazzled. I felt very happy to be part of the celebrations – something I would have missed had I remained in France.

Chapter 30

A LIFE-CHANGING ENCOUNTER

IN SEPTEMBER OF THAT YEAR, a chance meeting one morning at Westland Row Railway Station was about to change my life and would leave an enduring, indelible mark for the future. I was on my way to work and had just alighted from the train from Balbriggan. My heart skipped a beat when among the crowds on the platform, I spied a black-clad figure who I recognised as my dear schooldays-friend, Tommy Connor. Not having seen each other for over ten years, we were both happy to greet each other. He explained that he was now living in the headquarters of the Salesian Order in Dublin. He was in a hurry to catch another train but wanted to know if he could call me. I shouted after him that our phone number was in the telephone directory. I understood that he was still part of the Salesian Order and that he would have taken the same vows of poverty, chastity and obedience as nuns, and that his studies would ultimately lead to ordination to the priesthood. A few days later, he called me at home for a chat. I was surprised to hear him ask me if I would visit him.

Excited that a long-lost friend had suddenly reappeared into my life, I arrived at Salesian House in St Teresa's Road in Crumlin bearing a little gift of a porcelain candle holder and was ushered into a parlour where we chatted for over an hour. He accompanied me back to the bus stop, and we bid each other farewell. But that was not the end of it. He would ring me to arrange a meeting, and we would meet up regularly for long walks in the city. It was just as if time had rolled back and we were young teenagers again, exactly as it had been after choir practice so many years ago. So much had happened in our lives since then. There was no physical contact whatsoever. We just chatted, joked and laughed, enjoying each other's company. Our conversations were punctuated by long silences during which we just walked along the Royal Canal and in the streets of Dublin. We occasionally discussed religion, but seldom anything else of a serious nature. I loved him dearly and had done so from the first day that I had met him in Keeling's dairy, wearing his First Communion suit. I loved him when we were teenagers going for long walks. Now, both aged in our late twenties, he was a much-loved friend. I admired his intellect and his serious take on life, but I had no desire to be anything more than friends with him. His friendship was precious to me. I could confide in him about my struggle with the Faith, the Catholic Church and anything else that might be troubling me. I knew that he could be trusted with my innermost beliefs or doubts. During our walks, I was totally unaware of any inner struggles that might have been assailing him. At no time did he ever mention any problem or turmoil, either physical or spiritual. I took this as a sign of his contentment and commitment to the path in life he had taken.

Many months passed, and sometimes I would not hear from him. I was still in a relationship with John and continuing to enjoy my newfound freedom and independence. I certainly never dreamed that very soon, another event would complicate my life. Enjoying my evening meal lovingly cooked for me by my mother, which she always had ready when I arrived home from work, I was surprised to get a phone call from Tommy. He was calling from his parent's home in Balbriggan. Well, rather from their next-door neighbour's phone. He was very upset, telling me that his father had died suddenly on that day. I said I would like to call up to the house. His father was reposing at his home, laid out in the usual Irish Catholic way so that family and friends could pay their respects and sympathise with the bereaved. He told me that he would meet me at his front gate. When I arrived, Tommy was waiting at the gate. He made it obvious that he did not want me to go into the house. I was not prepared for the clanger he would drop. Still standing outside with his arms resting on the front gate, we chatted and after I had sympathised with him and said how sorry I was for his loss, he just blurted out that he was leaving the religious life. To say I was shocked and surprised is putting it mildly. A thousand questions went through my mind. He had never even hinted that he was unhappy or disillusioned in his vocation. Mumbling and stuttering, I told him that grief and bereavement could do strange things to people. He sounded adamant, however, that he had made up his mind. My mind raced. I really wondered how or when this would happen. Where would he go? What would he do? I decided it was none of my business, and I went off home.

In the summer of 1967, a local curate, Fr. O'Brien, started a savings scheme in a vacant old cottage in Mill Street Balbriggan. Called the Credit Union, it was to be run mainly by volunteers and was intended to replace moneylenders, loan sharks and the use of Hire Purchase schemes to buy household goods. In those days, a moneylender called Mr White was a regular visitor to the town. A long-nosed gentleman, wearing a brown felt trilby hat, he called to all the houses in the street, offering household items or a cheque to purchase clothes in Clerys store in Dublin. He would collect payment in instalments that seemed to last forever. The Credit Union (La Caisse Populaire) had started in Canada and had a greater impact on the town than was expected. It still flourishes to this day. Although its principle is simple (shares could be bought and were used to lend out money to others), it was greeted with scepticism by some people. But for me, it opened up a new way of thinking; I could now afford to travel to places I had only previously dreamed of.

Weeks passed. The new year began, and at the end of January 1969, I received a birthday card and a letter from Tommy. He was in London and staying with his sister until he found employment. I answered his letter. He would ring me from time to time. I was anxious to know how he would survive in such a big city. I wondered how he would adapt to life outside of the monastery. We hadn't seen each other for nearly a year when I arranged a visit to my friend Blanche in Highgate, London.

Tommy was delighted when I let him know that I would be visiting London shortly. He sounded happy and told me he would meet me at Heathrow Airport. Looking forward to seeing him again, I was thrilled and excited. I bought a new outfit – a navy dress and jacket trimmed with a yellow floral material and a straw hat. The trip would last two weeks, and I would be staying in Highgate with Blanche.

Blanche Osborn, previously called Sister de la Compassion, with whom I had worked in the Roquette prison, had returned to London at the age of 57 and had contacted me. It was the start of a friendship that would last for more than thirty years. Her courage, resilience, determination, and independent outlook on life were a constant example for me. Having spent 20 years working in the prison, she left the religious life to go back to England and was able to obtain employment in the administration department of the British Museum. Her ground floor flat in Highgate was an oasis of peace and tranquillity whenever I visited her. Her Mini Morris Minor was converted to hand controls because of a shorter right leg. This was a constant reminder of having suffered polio as a small child. Because of this, she wore a heavy surgical boot.

My transition from life in religion to independent living is due in no small measure to her example. She painted watercolours in her spare time. Her pictures of flowers were beautiful, delicate and showed real talent. Before her entry into religious life, she had had a live-in relationship during WWII with a Polish immigrant, had converted to Catholicism and had studied art at Battersea College of Art. It was there she became acquainted with a male model called Quintin Crisp, who had been arrested and charged for loitering in the streets of London. He had openly portrayed his homosexuality by his eccentric fashion, heavy theatrical make-up and his flamboyant demeanour. Blanche was called as a witness at his trial. She limped into the witness box and spoke of him as her friend and pleaded for leniency on his behalf. This scene is recalled in the screen adaptation of Crisp's book *The Naked Civil Servant*.

When Tommy met me at the airport, we went straight to Peckham in South London. Deliriously happy to see each other again, we held hands as we boarded the train to his sister Peggy's house. She had a meal ready and left us alone in the lounge to enjoy our reunion. When evening came, and it would be necessary for me to take two trains to Highgate, it was suggested we wait until morning. We would have to sleep on the lounge floor with a blanket to cover us. This inconvenience and lack of comfort did not bother me, and I just lay down fully clothed. Shoes were the only items removed as we slept or tried to doze off. The next day, Sunday, we headed to the nearest Catholic church for Mass and then proceeded to Highgate.

Tommy had got a job in a financial institution in Edgware. He was looking for a room to rent near the office. I was so happy that he now had a job and could support himself. We saw a lot of each other during those two weeks, mostly at Blanche's flat. They got on very well together as they were intelligent, well-educated and were able to discuss topics of mutual interest. During the days when both were working, I went shopping and sightseeing. I fell in love with London. It was springtime, and the daffodils were in bloom in the parks and gardens. A feeling that it would be nice to live in such a vibrant city began to take hold in my thoughts. Before the second week ended, I had applied for a job in London at Sea Containers Inc.

Arriving for the interview, I was immediately impressed with their offices in Park Street, which ran parallel to Hyde Park. The interview with HR went well, even though I was not up to scratch for the typing test. The company accountant needed a secretary, and the typing would be correspondence and a lot of typing of statistics. Two days later, a phone call to Blanche's telephone, followed by a letter, confirmed that my application had been successful. The starting date would be in one month's time.

Back home, I handed in my notice to my employer and began packing up both my belongings and my relationship with John. The excitement I was feeling at the prospect of living in London overrode any consideration for my family or John's feelings. I took no notice of any negative comments. Any chagrin in departing was alleviated by the prospect of independence and security.

The starting salary with Sea Containers would be one hundred pounds sterling per calendar month. This was a big step up from the forty pounds I was getting in Dublin. Being near Tommy would also be a bonus.

Arriving in London in July 1969 was an exciting time for me. For the very first time in my life, I would live alone independently and be financially self-sufficient. First and foremost, I had to find accommodation. I found a room in a woman's hostel in Islington. Being a very old building, it resembled an army camp or a prison. It was run on a strictly regimental basis: no male visitors, and lights had to be out at 10 pm. Gates were locked, and no exit or admittance was allowed after that time. After about three weeks there, I answered an ad to live with an Irish family, with free lodgings in return for some babysitting and housework. Tommy came with me to see what this entailed. When we got to the London Borough Council flat, we were greeted with a strong smell of urine, nicotine and onions. The place was a complete shamble of clothes everywhere, food scattered on tables, cupboards yawning to reveal everything from a needle to an anchor. Five young children sat around the room, screaming, crying and fighting. I felt sorry for the poor mother who had a cigarette hanging from her lips in her tired and worn-out face. We retreated, saying I would "think about it." Once outside, Tommy was the first to speak.

"That's some dungeon".

I didn't need much time to think about it. I never went back there and refused the offer. The next visit to possible digs was in Seven Sisters Road. This was a furnished bedsit in an owner-occupied house, situated in a leafy garden at five pounds per week rent. I was happy here in spite of the landlady's little yappy dog who greeted me each evening. The barking would alert her to my comings and goings. She would emerge to check whether I was accompanied or not. On weekends if Tommy arrived, he was to wait below in the hallway until

I was ready to go out with him. Therefore, ruling out the possibility of any intimacy.

Starting work in Sea Containers Inc. was wonderful. Such a beautiful building! Carpeted with beige wool carpets throughout, there was a staff room with a large well-stocked fridge containing a free supply of soft drinks. The male and female staff occupying offices on three floors were all British. It was a pleasure to arrive each morning, and I soon got to know everyone by name. The receptionist at the front desk greeted me, and we chatted for a while each day. She would invite me to lunch, as she knew all the nice cafés. My boss, Tony Dearden, would ask me to bring back a cream cheese and cucumber sandwich. The receptionist was called Beatrice Hughes, and we became lifelong friends. She was younger than I and had a great sense of fun. I loved the shops at Marble Arch. The freedom to browse in Selfridges and other stores on Oxford Street was wonderful. Fashion and jewellery called out to me from shop windows. Lured in by thoughts of arriving home to Balbriggan all dressed up, I browsed in Harrods and bought a little jar of mustard just to be seen with their carrier bag. I was getting snobbish!

I now had a bank account in Barclays bank and a cheque book! Such a comeuppance in the world, from cash in an old used envelope back in Dublin. What a change from the vow of poverty! I budgeted carefully and was able to send money home, which was expected in those days. Bea and I went to pubs and parties on the weekends. Life was idyllic. Petticoat Lane and Portobello markets were among our favourite haunts. Unable to emulate the London accent, I was recognised as Irish wherever I went. In spite of this, I felt integrated into London life. Tommy, however…I felt he was still struggling with the fact that he was now out in the big world and did not have the structured framework of monastic life in which to feel secure. His spirituality was being tested, and he was being influenced by his family, especially his stepmother, back in Ireland. Although we never discussed finances, I was aware that he felt responsible for her in some way now that she was alone since his father had gone. His detachment from the reality of life in London was apparent as he didn't participate in any social activity. Our meetings consisted of visits to Blanche, Mass on Sundays and walks in the streets or parks. This did not bother me as I was content to be able to kiss and hug him lovingly, to be in his company, and to daydream during his long periods of silence. In addition to not being committed, I was totally free to live my own life, which I jolly well did!

In the meantime, I had moved into a house at 9 Maud Road, Leyton in East London, sharing with the landlord, who worked in the mailroom at Sea Containers. Having inherited the house from his aunt, John Jackson was a tall, incredibly handsome six-footer in his forties. He was single and was fanatical about cleanliness. We got along really well as long as I kept my distance. I still had those dreadful nightmares. Woken by my screams, he would appear at my bedroom door with a mighty sabre, thinking that I was being attacked by an intruder. He did not have a car but had a bicycle. He took me to junk sales in the East End, where I was able to buy an old black bike, which I rode with him all around Epping Forest. We visited many places of historical interest, and I appreciated his wisdom and knowledge.

In spite of the wonderful life I was leading in London, I missed my family. My mother wrote lovely newsy letters to me, and I called her on the telephone as often as possible. Thinking of John often, I sent him a card for his birthday in October of that year. Replying with a long letter, he expressed the wish to come to visit London to see me and also that he would love to see his favourite soccer team Tottenham play. His visit was arranged to coincide with a big match, and I looked forward to seeing somebody from home.

I had a wonderful time during the long weekend of John's visit. He had travelled by boat to Holyhead, where he had taken the train to London. I was there to meet him on his arrival at Euston Station. The first thing he wanted was a drink in the nearest pub.

Life in London continued to be great. I knew my way around the Underground and enjoyed visiting places of interest on weekends. My brother Malachy's wedding to Joyce was coming up, so I booked a journey to Ireland by train and ship via Holyhead. It was great to be home for that occasion and to see all my family. The wedding was held in Rush Church, and Joyce's five sisters were bridesmaids.

Joyce and I reminisced about the trip to the west of Ireland we had made some years previously – hitchhiking from Galway to Donegal, visiting Glenties, Adara, Killybegs, staying in B&Bs along the way. From Killybegs, we got a jaunt in a small fishing boat to the Island of Arranmore off the Donegal coast. There we had tea at the only hotel. This was served in a silver teapot with bone china cups and dainty sandwiches. It cost us the princely sum of two shillings and sixpence each. We returned to the mainland in the same little fishing boat, and from there, we made our way to Glencolumbkille. It was there that I had one of my worst nightmares. Sharing a twin bedroom with Joyce, I woke up on the floor. I had fallen out of bed, screaming. The next morning the man of the house, while serving breakfast, apologised to us, saying that he hoped that we had not been disturbed by the noisy crowd going home from the pub, adding that some women have no shame screaming in the street when they should be at home in their bed. Neither Joyce nor I admitted that it was my screams that had woken him, but we had a good laugh afterwards. We moved on from there and made our way to Letterkenny, thumbing our way in vans, cars, cattle trucks, and trailers. Passing through Northern Ireland, we arrived in Monaghan, where we knocked at Joyce's cousin's house and were welcomed to a meal and rest for the night. Ah, it had been one of my best memories.

Back in London, Tommy and I continued seeing each other. He loved cricket, so we spent a whole day at the Oval cricket ground watching an international match. Even though I knew nothing about cricket, I was happy to be there with him because I loved him. My love for him was pure adoration and admiration. I admired his integrity, his wisdom and his maturity beyond his years. I accepted and believed everything he did or said. Whatever he decided to do, I blindly went along with it, wherever and whenever. Sharing our hopes and dreams, we often discussed our relationship with God. I never questioned whether my love was reciprocated; I just presumed it was. When he teased me about my lack of faith, my bad language, or my being always late, we laughed together, and I lived in a never-ending state of joy and happiness. On one occasion during Sunday Mass, while we were listening to the priest's sermon, to my great astonishment, Tommy stood up shouting "Rubbish" and quickly marched down the aisle, making a quick exit. Needless to say, I did not follow him. When Mass ended, I found him sitting in the nearby garden of the crematorium in Golders Green. I knew he would be there, as when the weather was fine, we would sit there together admiring the flowers. Tommy would have a smoke. He smoked a lot; it was his sole extravagance.

Feeling a little guilty that I had not mentioned John's visit, I did not dare tell him that we had spent a night in a hotel room in the same bed. Not that much had happened that night. We had been to the pub and were both inebriated when we checked in. John had given our fictitious address as 19 Upper Dorset Street Dublin, while I flashed a brass ring, bought from a market stall, on my wedding ring finger. The previous day on Brighton Beach, he had asked me to marry him, or rather suggested marriage. It certainly was not a formal proposal on bended knees. I replied that I would think about it. I was still thinking about it when I fell asleep beside him in the hotel room in Central London. Sex before marriage was a taboo subject back then. Nobody ever admitted to it except when the obvious outcome appeared nine months later. It was considered a mortal sin and still is – if one is to be faithful to the Church's teaching. Needless to say, the subject was never part of the conversation between Tommy and me. It would have been unthinkable to even discuss such matters unless it was in relation to procreation within the sacrament of marriage.

It was at this point that I began to seriously realise that Tommy was not adjusting to everyday life outside of the religious framework at the same pace as I was. This sometimes irritated me to the extent that I kept quiet when he would sound preachy about the dangers of alcohol, modern music or short skirts. Religion seemed to constantly come between us. Whereas I had been to see the musical *Oh Calcutta*, which was unbelievably explicit – naked males prancing around the stage, a row of naked men with their backs to the audience getting excited while watching pornography on a big screen in front of them – Tommy had not at this point shaken off the shackles of his past and would have been outraged at such shenanigans.

Thoughts of home invariably included John. I missed him terribly. It was hard to imagine life without him. His wit and attitude to life always made me happy to be in his company. I wondered how and why he was still interested in me after I had left him to go to work in London. I thought about the times we had spent together in the company of our friends, remembering the night we went with Teddy Welsh and Donny Bissett to a dance in Bray where Joe Dolan and his band were playing. Donny had met a girl called Margaret from Crumlin, and we collected her and her friend before heading off to Bray. We had a wonderful night dancing and listening to the great crooner. A visit to the chipper followed, and it was past 2 am before we deposited Margaret home. Her friend couldn't remember the number of the house where she was staying. She was on holiday from the US and didn't know the locality very well. It took John hours to drive around housing estates trying to get her home. It was daybreak when I got home to be met on the doorstep by my mother, who was ready to send out a search party for me.

Doubts about having a future with Tommy came to a head while we were on one of our usual walks, and the conversation turned to whether his family knew about our friendship. He revealed that he never mentioned me at all to his stepmother. I asked him why that was, and his reply shocked me. I was speechless. He informed me that she had warned him that I was a bad influence because, to quote her words, "she drinks". I said nothing, but those two words kept repeating in my head. They began to fester. Deeply hurt and feeling that Tommy agreed with her and that he was deeply influenced by her, I began to realise that their allegiance to the Pioneer Total Abstinence Association amounted to bigotry. Weeks passed. We continued to see each other, but the spark had gone out for me. Enough was enough. On saying goodnight to each other one evening in the London Underground, we both knew it was over. I said goodbye. We turned in different directions: him to catch a train on the northern line, and I headed to my connection on the central line. We never saw each other again in London. Nor did we speak or contact each other again. To lose a friend is always heart-breaking. He was the only person from home in the great big city of London that I thought I could rely on. He had been a link for me to Balbriggan, the Church and to God. That was all gone now. It became obvious to me that it was probably a relief for him to live his own life without any attachment. His high standards and ideals were no longer relevant to me. Eventually, my heart healed somewhat in the knowledge that he was progressing in his employment in a financial institution. Although I was bitterly disappointed that Tommy made no sign nor effort to keep in touch, I consoled my heavy heart and accepted that my feelings had not been reciprocated. On the other hand, for me, it was another chapter setting me free of the constraints of religion. It was with a tremendous feeling of liberation that I began to see life in a totally different light. Now free to make the best of my life independently in London as an adult, and breaking out of my cocoon, a truly wonderful metamorphosis began to unfold.

From somewhere within me, a need to visit Baldock again emerged and kept niggling me. Was this an unconscious desire to prove to myself that I was not a social misfit or to let the nuns know that I was not a total failure? Perhaps it was both. Bea agreed with enthusiasm to come with me on the short train trip to revisit the nuns and the convent in Baldock. We set out one bright Sunday morning. I had dressed modestly in my best outfit. Alas, Bea arrived at the station in a pair of hot pants, which were all the fashion. Her dark skin was glistening with the latest make-up, and her hair was straightened into a ponytail. What a spectacle we must have presented to the Sister who opened the door to us. Many years had passed since I had arrived there aspiring to religious life. I did not recognise anyone living there. The reception we received was both polite and frosty, and our visit did not last long. We laughed long and hard on our way back to London. That was how we spent most of our time – just laughing and giggling, making fun of the world around us. Bea lived in a very posh area of London. Holland Park Avenue was a leafy upmarket zone. She lived with her parents, who were of Indian origin, in a four-story Georgian house with steps leading up to the front door. Bea fancied a young man who worked at the Underground station. After much eyelash flashing and the odd wink, she had clinched a date with him, but this did not interfere with our friendship, nor did it shorten the time we spent together at markets and window gazing.

Around this time, a male colleague in Sea Containers asked me out on a date. We went to see *Ryan's Daughter*. I cried throughout the film. As soon as I heard the theme music and saw the scenes that were filmed in Ireland, the floodgates opened. I had trouble lowering the sound of my slobbery sobs. Any romance with the fellow beside me fizzled out before it even began. When the lights went up, my scarf and the sleeves of my coat were soddened with tears. I knew I needed to get home to Balbriggan.

Life in London was wonderful. It was a great place to be young and healthy. Working and socialising made the time go by at an amazing speed. On the other hand, time dragged along slowly. To me, it seemed like ages since I had seen my family. John wrote letters, and we spoke often on the phone. He would relate some of the local news, how his work was going and anything happening in his family. He wanted to know how I was getting on. I thought long and hard about what married life with John would be like. To have someone close who really cared about me and who I could love and cherish for the rest of my life seemed a great possibility. I prayed for guidance. Slowly but surely, I realised that home with John was where I really wanted to be. This conviction took up residence in my mind. On one particular day, when I rang his home phone number, his sister answered, telling me he was not at home. She asked me if she could give him a message. "Yes," I replied, "Tell him the answer is yes". As any phone calls home to Ireland had to be made from a call box in the street, I said that I would call the following evening. That was the way I replied to his proposal. The next day he was waiting for my call and was delighted. I could hear it in his voice. Many questions and answers were exchanged until I ran out of coins for the coin box in the telephone kiosk.

As it was coming up to Christmas, we decided that we would become engaged on my next visit. Sea Containers where I still worked were having their Christmas staff party on the same night that I had booked a flight home to Dublin.

John met me at the airport on that Christmas Eve morning. We went straight away to Des Byrne's jeweller shop on Bachelors Walk, Dublin, to buy an engagement ring. A dainty solitaire diamond in a very unusual setting caught my eye. On my finger, it looked so beautiful that all the other rings seemed like knuckle dusters. This was the ring that I would wear for the rest of my life. I had to have it. It cost 69 pounds, and after lunch in Clerys top floor restaurant, we went home to tell my parents. As I breezed into the house, flashing the ring, everyone was very happy. We planned to get married in June of the following year. In order to save money for the wedding, I would return to my job in London until then. John was such a lovable person, and I was in love with him. Reliable, trustworthy, honest and a hard worker, it was great to feel comfortable and relaxed in his company. The premises of his place of work had been sold to Tierney Bros, and he continued to pay rent and to manage his own business of car sales and repairs until the building was sold on to a tyre company who wanted the premises to be vacated. This disaster meant that the sales and repairs could no longer occupy the premises, and preparations were made for a restart in an unused barn in Clonard Street. John was also driving cabs with Tolan Taxis.

Leaving my job in Sea Containers, saying goodbye to my friends Blanche and Bea, I promised to keep in touch. I parcelled up my wedding dress onto the back of my old boneshaker bicycle. With mutton sleeves, this high-necked creation with covered buttons and a curved train would sweep the ground behind me on my big day. My landlord John Jackson cycled to Euston Station on my bicycle, complete with the wedding dress tied on the carrier while I followed by bus. I took the train to Holyhead with the bike in the guard's carriage. My mother and John greeted me in Dun Laoghaire when I came ashore wheeling my bike. It was my second homecoming. But what a difference this reunion was to when I had arrived from France a few years previously. On this occasion, I was filled with joy and happiness.

Chapter 31

MARRIED LIFE

JOHN AND I WERE MARRIED in St Peter and Paul's Church, Balbriggan, on the 5th of June 1971, with my sisters Frances and Claire as my bridesmaids. Mrs Collins from Craoibhin Park made their maxi length floral dresses. John's brother Barney and his nephew Brian were his best men. My nieces Grainne and Fiona were tiny flower girls. My father and I were the last to leave the house in Drogheda Street, and except for remarking that it was a beautiful day, we did not exchange many words. Arriving at the church and emerging from the taxi, I was surprised to see a crowd of local ladies standing waiting to see the bride. As soon as I entered the door of the church, I knew I was in trouble in the shoe department. Clinging on for dear life to my father's arm, I tottered forth to the strains of the organist pounding out "Here Comes the Bride". My shoes were too tight, and the spindle heels almost caused two sprained ankles. In spite of this discomfort, I felt blissfully happy. This was my special day. I was about to begin a new life. Looking forward to being John's wife, having a family and a home to call our own was exciting, and knowing that I was the centre of attention, really led me to believe that the world was beautiful and that nothing would ever be difficult again.

All my aunts, uncles and some of my cousins were in the church dressed in new clothes, complete with hats and gloves for the occasion. These were seated on the left-hand side, while John's sisters, Tess McGuinness, Claire Cronin, and Finn Rock, congregated together with his mother Julia, accompanied by John's brother Ultan on the right-hand side. Many friends and neighbours from both families were also invited. The reception was held at the Old Shieling Hotel in Raheny. As the wedding Mass was over at midday, everyone was famished with hunger and thirst when we got to the hotel. During his speech, my father mentioned that as I was the last of the girls in the family to be wed – and alluding to panning for gold – that John was fortunate to have found the precious metal at the bottom of the pan. Flattered by his words, I realised that he held me in high esteem. Music followed soon after the meal, and John and I (in a pair of borrowed flat sandals) took to the floor for the customary first dance. The Flemings family band proceeded to play lively tunes, and most of the guests joined us on the dancefloor.

After the reception, John and I flew to the island of Jersey on our honeymoon. This island in the English Channel with beautiful scenery, a clear sky, gorgeous food, and crystal blue sea provided us with two weeks of blissful enjoyment and rest. After the honeymoon, we came back to live in our two-roomed flat on the top floor of Laragh House in Church St. We shared this floor with another couple – John and Gay Kavanagh (Halligan), who also occupied two rooms. With our many wedding presents, we furnished our rooms comfortably and stylishly. We snuggled between rich Foxford wool blankets and a lavish eiderdown, dined from fine English bone china, and tread on plush carpet mats. John rocked in his rocking chair while gazing proudly at his mother's present of a china cabinet, bursting with gifts of crystal and cutlery.

We then rented a house in Station Street in Balbriggan for a year. When Fancourt Heights housing estate was being built, we applied for a local authority loan to purchase number 101. We borrowed £5250 from Dublin County Council, having gathered the deposit of £500. It was our home for 27 years. During this time, our two daughters, Catherine and Joanne, brought great joy to John and me. Unfortunately, our marriage began to show cracks in the early 1980s and finally collapsed, leaving me alone with two young children and a mortgage. Many challenges lay ahead.

Some years later, while Joanne and Catherine were attending St Theresa's Primary School, we moved into a townhouse in the centre of Balbriggan. In groups of four attached houses, Lawless and Gibbons Terrace is named after the two local men who were brutally killed by the Black and Tans in 1920. Moving here provided us with a great group of neighbours of different ages and occupations. Built in 1937 by the Town Commissioners, the houses had been allocated to local young couples and their families. Many of these families or their descendants were still living there when we moved into 15 Gibbons Terrace. We enjoyed chatting with the locals over the garden wall. The lady next door regaled us with descriptions and stories of her childhood during both world wars.

The 1980s and 90s passed very quickly. My children's school days were very busy. They joined Mrs Gibbons' dancing classes, the brass and reed band, and the Girl Guides. Summers were always a welcome break. Time spent swimming and lazing on the back beach were very happy times. My sisters and I relived the happy days that we enjoyed on the flat banks when we were children with Mammy and Basie. Now we had our own children: Claire had married Tommy Sweetman, and she had David, Karen, Robert and Rosie. Frances would come on holidays from Dublin with Niall, Raymond and Áine. We had picnics at the old bath house beside the Martello tower – our favourite haunt. Back in the 50s, the now derelict building had been a popular venue for hot seawater baths. Steam could be seen gushing out of the chimney. While standing at the door, Katie Dunne welcomed people from far and wide for the "cure", and Mr Carney collected seaweed in buckets of seawater to fill the boilers for the baths.

While our children swam and played in the sand, we adults sunned ourselves, exchanged tittle-tattle and watched people coming and going with their families and pets. Flasks of tea replaced the teapot on the fire. Old friendships were nurtured, and new friends were made. The Sunshiners still arrived in procession with their leaders, interrupting the laid-back atmosphere with their gleeful singing and excited shouting.

It was during this era that the Balbriggan Breakaway Festivals were held. Dressing up for the parade at the start of the week-long festivities caused lots of excitement. Great fun was had at the barman's race, the mini-marathon, and the competitions for Miss Balbriggan and Glamorous Grandmother. Fabulous prizes were offered to the winner of the Bachelor of the Year competition. Pat Hickey was the proud winner in 1987. Tom Murphy had taken the prize the previous year. It was at this time I took up running. It started when Aidan Brennan announced that he would coach anyone interested in doing the festival mini-marathon. A swarm of women and young people turned up for his exercise routines on the green area in Lambeecher. We started trotting in groups of various abilities. On one practice run, I stopped by to see my father. His eyes widened when he saw me in shorts for the first time. Throwing his eyes up to heaven, he exclaimed:

"I hope no one saw you coming in here dressed like that!"

I just laughed and knew that he was only joking. Incidentally, the shorts reached well down to my knees and were very loose.

My friend Marie and I got breathless at Flemington Lane. Aches and pains followed the next day. Encouraged by Aidan, we persevered. Our fitness levels increased, and we turned up at the starter line. The sun was shining as we made our way through Grugha, Delahasey and back down by Clonard Cross. I won a prize for the first competitor over 40 years old to finish. Any physical discomfort lingering in my muscles was well compensated by the feeling of fitness and wellbeing experienced at the end of a training run.

In 1988, when I was asked to write a contribution to the Breakaway Festival programme, I remembered that way back in the late 1940s, a bedraggled and odd-looking individual roamed the streets of Balbriggan. Her appearance depicted wretchedness and vagrancy. For the children playing outside, she incited fear and terror, and they scrambled indoors at the sight of her. This provoked her to shout and roar obscenities. Her clothes were unrecognisable as such. Old rags and sackcloth covered her in winter and in summer. Great tufts of matted grey hair pushed their way out from under a thick woollen headscarf. Her black boots with no laces, too big for her feet, made a clip-clop noise as she shuffled through the streets. Most of all, it was her wild facial expression that made children run in the opposite direction. She didn't belong to the travelling community or the tinkers who arrived regularly into town. Knocking on doors, she begged and gathered whatever she could to survive. Not many people answered her call. My mother always kept a sixpence or a threepenny piece on the mantelpiece for Bessie. She'd go to a patch of waste ground at the end of our street, make a fire and boil up water for her nettle tea.

I wrote the following which appeared in the Festival programme.

Ode to Bessie Baw

Oh oft, when in my bed I lie,
I dwell on times gone by.
I think about the times gone past.
And thoughts go through my head.
Of Corcoran's Hill, of Gallen's Mill.
Just bear with me awhile.
Walk 'round the Head and up the hill,
The children laugh "haw haw",
"Ah, there goes Bessie Baw."

The boats are in, and here comes Jemmer.

Now long gone from us, but I remember.
The cod, the flatfish, herrings galore.
The poor got plenty, Bessie and many more.
God rest you and Bessie Baw.
Now Smyco is gone, and Hampton Mills,
The rich all dead; they left no wills.
No jobs, no money, less ringing of the tills.
But let's not be sad that times are bad.
Life's not so dull; the pubs are full.
And there are Bessies still among us.

So, if from Balbriggan you have gone,

To find a fortune fair,
Then seek no more.

Married Life

Come back! We're still the same.

Ah, there's Bessie at the door.

Following publication, the matter of this article came up for discussion on the agenda of the local Council. Councillor Jack Kirby put forward a motion calling on the members to lodge a complaint with the Breakaway Festival committee and the parish priest, stating that the mention of the said disreputable name was offensive and should remain in oblivion. The Chairman proposed a vote. Someone at the table muttered the words of Jesus: "Let he who is without sin cast the first stone".

After this, I made some enquiries. Bessie O'Brien had been a beautiful young woman at the time of the war of independence. She had formed a relationship with one of the British soldiers billeted in nearby Gormanston Army camp. To have sided with the Black and Tans was deemed a crime. From then on, Bessie was ostracised, spat upon and called White Rabbit. Treated as an outcast, her reputation ruined, and disowned by her family; she became unemployable and homeless for the rest of her life. She died in a mental institution and was buried in an unmarked grave.

In spite of struggling as a sole parent, Catherine and Joanne had always given me lots of motivation. During this time, I felt frustrated that my knowledge of French was being wasted, and I didn't have an up-to-date formal qualification to make use of my ability to speak, read and write this European language. When Ireland became a member of the European Union in 1992, there was an increased demand in schools and businesses for French teachers and interpreters. Eventually, I decided to do something about my lack of confidence and initiative. At 54 years of age, having applied and been accepted for a course in Dublin City University, off I went each day by bus equipped with a pencil, paper and a few reference books. It was tough going. Without knowing it at the time, my hearing was beginning to fail. Struggling at lectures to understand the intricacies of phonetics, my assignments came back riddled with red ink. I would return home tired, disheartened and ready to give up. However, in addition to thinking of the hard-earned cash that had paid my fee and the example I wished to give my daughters, determination and willpower spurred me on. At the end of the course, I sat for the Examinations in Languages for International Communication and was awarded the Advanced Certificate by the Institute of Linguists Educational Trust, London. Armed with this newfound confidence, I was able to work in Dublin for a French Company with headquarters in Paris. My daughters, who were both learning the language in school, and had stayed many times in Beauvais, France, were doing well in the language. While tutoring them, I was learning a lot about the curriculum and the required standards for secondary school French exams. This enabled me to help other students to prepare for their Junior and Leaving Certificates. Adults preparing for interviews sought my help, and I was able to tutor an Air Traffic Controller and a future Irish Ambassador. This was a very happy and rewarding period in my life. It made me realise that my stay in religious life had had some compensation. After primary school, Catherine and Joanne both attended Loreto Secondary School and went on to obtain university degrees. During the school holidays, we travelled to England and France. My friendship with Marie France and her husband Gerard enabled us to travel to Beauvais, France, many times and to invite each of their four children to sojourn in Balbriggan to perfect their English. We visited Joanne's godmother in Spain. In addition to many visits to London to see my friends Blanche and Bea, with whom we have always kept in touch, Iceland was another memorable trip we made. It was, therefore, inevitable that both of my girls would become infected with the travel bug.

Part 4

Chapter 32

YEARS LATER…

LOOKING BACK OVER THE PAST can be bittersweet. Whichever way I choose to look back over my life, it can be either exhilarating or depressing. I can do nothing to change the past. Sometimes I ask myself if I was able to relive those years, what would I do differently? The results of soul searching and deliberating might throw up lots of regrets or guilt. I prefer to dwell on wonderful memories and happy times. I have come to understand that the major decisions I have taken were made with the best of intentions at the time. If entering religious life at the young age of seventeen sounds incongruous or out of place in this day and age, it certainly was not the case back in 1959. Ireland at that time was a far cry from what it is today. Uninfluenced by modern technology or media, religion was more than just a practice of what we believed in. It was embedded in our culture; it was a way of life. Therefore, commitment to vows in religious life was a natural progression from promises and the Pledge made at Confirmation, in the Girl Guides, and even by partaking in regular confession in the Sacrament of Penance when one resolved to sin no more. For many young people, the next step was to join a teaching, nursing or missionary congregation.

It never ceases to amaze me how people, especially men, are curious about nuns and ex-nuns. From embarrassing questions and lewd jokes, nuns are often the subject of comedy and ridicule. Many people are intrigued as to why a woman would give up her life to God and to the service of others. It was never my intention to expand on this episode of my life, but I must admit that my experience within religious life has had a tremendous impact and has left a lasting effect that can never be erased. God knows, I tried to forget it ever happened. My reluctance to discuss the subject was never a question of regret. It was just something I've always felt was private and unique to me. There are some things we cannot discuss with others. Perhaps for me, it was the fear of being judged a failure or an oddball, and my struggle with faith and religion was difficult enough without intrusion from outsiders.

Many changes have occurred in Ireland that have had an impact on my outlook and on our everyday way of life. Two of the most important changes spring to mind. Firstly, when Ireland voted for the Maastricht Treaty in 1992, 69% of the population voted in favour, and Taoiseach Albert Reynolds secured 8 billion euros in aid for development and infrastructure. Joining the European Union also meant freedom of movement for people of all nations within the Union. Ireland then needed migrant workers to build houses and construct roads. They came from Poland, Lithuania, and other Eastern Bloc countries. The Celtic Tiger was born. Money was available for developers to buy up land and create private housing estates. Banks made loans available for mortgages to first-time buyers, and house owners upgraded their properties and bought holiday homes on the Continent. The Government set up an employment service called FÁS. This initiative enabled the long-term unemployed to sign up for retraining courses and work placements while retaining their benefits. The standard of living rose dramatically. But most importantly, life for women improved. The pill and other forms of contraception became available. The hardships of frequent pregnancies and poverty that had been endured by past generations of women became less. Women were no longer obliged to remain in unhappy relationships, and in spite of the protestations of the Catholic Church, contraception, divorce, unmarried couples living together, single parenthood and homosexuality became acceptable.

While the troubles in Northern Ireland subsided somewhat after the Good Friday agreement signed on 10th April 1998, Ireland remained divided by the border separating six of the nine Counties of Ulster from the Republic of Ireland, which comprises 26 counties.

With the influx of foreign workers, immigrants and asylum seekers, the population continued to increase. With the need for schools and churches to expand, discontent crept into certain areas of society, with racism noticeably present in cities and small towns. Affluence grew as poverty diminished, and more and more people travelled abroad. As horizons widened, so too did people's minds. Other religions and beliefs were accepted into local communities. Little by little, the Catholic religion began to play a lesser role.

The second big change to shock the nation was the revelation on state television's popular Late Late Show, hosted by Gay Byrne in 1992, that Bishop Eamon Casey had fathered a son with an American woman. Annie Murphy told the audience that the Bishop of Galway was the father of her 18-year-old son. Shock and outrage followed. Every news bulletin carried the story. Newspapers were sold out with lightning speed. It was the start of a cleansing process within the Catholic Church. For the first time, a member of the clergy, who also held a position within the hierarchy, was exposed in a hypocritical light. At last, the victims of clerical abuse felt that they would be believed if they told their stories of suffering at the hands of paedophiles and perverts who paraded around appearing as paragons of virtue. A giant can of worms opened up. The country was outraged, and the scandals that emerged rocked the Catholic Church and tested the faith of many. For me, it was a tumultuous revelation. Confusion was mixed with anger. My childhood beliefs, aspirations and subsequent devotion to religious life seemed to have been useless and in vain. Conversations on the subject were rife, with people of all walks of life voicing their divided opinions.

One of the worst stories was that of Fr. Brendan Smyth. A notorious paedophile, he had been able to have access to children in care. Complaints made against priests had been covered up by the hierarchy who moved the perpetrators from one parish to another. Evil and criminal wrongdoings were never reported to the police. That all changed when Bishop Casey was exposed as a hypocrite who had also misappropriated Church monies to fund his love of fast cars and a lavish lifestyle. Thankfully, victims in Ireland and in other countries were now able to tell their stories and seek justice. The evil that has lain under the carpet of holiness was and still is being combed out like lice from an otherwise clean head. This is the way I look today at the church founded by Jesus. There are many good and holy priests and nuns who have dedicated their lives to the service of God and to humankind, and who have persevered in their vocation. It must be extremely difficult for these good and faithful men and women to be lumped together with those evil people and to be treated as being guilty by association.

While in the religious life, we were often lectured that those who did not persevere could be compared to rotten fruit falling from the tree. I have to refute this because I honestly believe that men and women who entered religion and then, for one reason or another did not continue, still made a difference to the lives of others, both while within the priesthood and convent life and also after they took paths in other directions. This was definitely the case for me. I had worked for many years solely for the glory of God; I had prayed and had made sacrifices. This devotion to God and to members of his flock left an indelible mark on my personality and my attitude to life. Never do unto others what you would not wish others to do unto you has always been my motto, and I am grateful for having had the experience of learning and of living in the religious life. I would also hope that my consideration for others continues to make a difference in our daily lives.

Vocations to the priesthood and religious life have diminished greatly in Ireland and elsewhere. Although members of Religious Orders now take a lesser role in secondary schools and hospitals, the majority of primary schools still have some input from the parish church. These and other changes have brought about a more open mentality. Other positive changes include the fact that owner-occupied homes are now the norm. Piping North Sea gas into Ireland was one of the greatest innovations, allowing central heating to be installed in most houses.

Thinking often of what my friend Tommy Connor would think of all this reminds me of the last time I saw and spoke to him. My friend Marmo had informed me that Tommy was terminally ill. He had returned to Ireland in the early 80s, had been employed in a Merchant Bank and had married. He was now a patient in a Dublin hospital. Marmo and I visited him two weeks before he lost his battle with mouth and throat cancer at the age of 36. He looked very handsome, sitting beside his bed dressed in a blue sweater and navy corduroy jeans as he greeted us warmly. I noticed that he had lost a lot of weight, but his lovely smile was still the same. I choked on the lump in my throat and tried to make conversation. As we were leaving, he walked to the top of the hospital stairs with us. I looked back up to see that he was still there, leaning on the rails. He smiled as I waved up to him.

When he died, he left a wife and two young children. I sometimes wonder if he knew of or suspected that evil lurked beneath the façade of the so-called perfection in religious life. His departure from the Order was sudden. Had he thought about it for a long time? Why had he become disillusioned? These questions often cross my mind as I remember his gentle manner and kindly smile.

One of the Dutch girls who had been in the Novitiate with me in Le Dorat and who had worked in Bordeaux had left the Order, contacted me and invited me to visit her in Eindhoven in Holland. My friend Sheila Loughry and I booked an Aer Lingus flight to Amsterdam, and we had a wonderful time with ex Sister Laetitia, now Miriam Claassen. We visited Volendam and the Zider Zee. It was the start of visits to more old friends who had left the Congregation.

I visited Blanche often and delighted in our discussions and debates on subjects ranging from the existence of God and the hereafter to the price of cat food for her pet, Tosca. She drove us on many shopping trips, outings to beautiful parks and the occasional day out to Brighton Beach. Her example of survival against the odds, against prejudice and preconceived ideas of ex-nuns, inspired me. Although I never consciously worried about how other people viewed my situation, I constantly strived to shed the utterly confusing, twisted threads of my life and to blank out the experience of having been away in a convent.

The reason I avoided talking about my years in France was a little bit like a returned war veteran; it would be too difficult for me to describe to someone who had not been through the same experience. For this reason, it was therapeutic to be able to talk openly with Blanche, and I owe her an immense debt in this respect.

Chapter 33

CURING OLD WOUNDS

TAKING THE FERRY FROM WEXFORD, I travelled many times to France on holiday. On one such visit, I went alone to the 11th arrondissement in Paris. Making my way to Rue de la Roquette, I was dumbstruck to see that the prison had been demolished. Words could not describe the mixed feelings, which left me spellbound. I resisted the urge to fling my arms in the air and to shout Hallelujah. On the other hand, I felt saddened that this historic building had been erased. The original large portal was all that remained at the entrance to a small park. Trees, flower beds and a skateboarding area made a pleasant change from the high black walls. Taking my place on one of the garden seats, memories came flooding back. Tears came to my eyes as I watched mothers stroll with children in buggies, elderly couples chatting or reading newspapers. I listened to the happy children playing on the swings and slides. What a contrast it was from scenes I had witnessed there in the past. The Sisters had been relocated to Fleury-Mérogis Prison in a suburb of Paris. I wondered how many of them remained. Who among them had left the Congregation or had died? I recalled the day John and I had travelled to County Meath for the funeral of one of Mother Superior's relatives. We had called to the house and had met her there. She showed no emotion whatsoever greeting me, but I was proud and pleased to let her know that I was happy and content in my life. Sitting now on the redeveloped site of the prison, I realised that for me, leaving and returning home had been the right thing to do. There was, however, another trip that I needed to make in order to dispel some negative feelings still lingering. I would go back to Le Dorat. In my heart of hearts, I knew it would be a very emotional journey that I was about to embark on alone. With nobody else to accompany me, I would face whatever lay ahead without further delay.

During the summer of 1996, 30 years had passed since I had last been to Le Dorat. I wondered what kind of reception I would get, and if anyone would remember me. Most of all, I needed to put any hang-ups away. I had been cruelly and completely cut off by Superiors from members of the Congregation with whom I had spent many years studying and working. Had I been cast away into oblivion by those same people? I needed answers, but had I left it too late? I wrote to the Reverend Mother General at the Motherhouse, telling her I would be in the region and would like to call. I booked two nights' bed and breakfast in an Auberge in Le Dorat. Travelling by train on that same journey from Paris to Le Dorat that I had made all those years ago, I recalled how young and naive I had been. Arriving at my destination, I stepped onto the platform and vividly remembered arriving there as a 17-year-old to be met by a Sister and Breda, who had transported my big suitcase in a wheelbarrow. As I walked towards the town, I noticed that nothing had changed except that there were a few more modern cars whizzing by. The spire of the 12th Century collegial loomed above the rest of the buildings, and as I got nearer to the centre of town, I passed the convent door on my way to the Auberge, which was an ancient, converted mansion with elegantly furnished rooms in the style of Louis XIV. That same afternoon I rang the doorbell at the main entrance to the convent, was ushered into a small parlour, and told that Mother would see me shortly. Then I suddenly realised that I had come all this way from Ireland totally unprepared and without any idea of what I was going to say or what to expect.

A middle-aged nun entered the room and greeted me warmly. She explained that she was originally a member of the Sisters of the Misericorde, who had amalgamated with the Sisters of Marie Joseph of the Prisons. She was very taken aback that I was able to converse with her in fluent French. We settled into a friendly conversation. She explained that due to dwindling numbers, the two Congregations of Les Soeurs de Marie Joseph des Prisons and Les Soeurs de la Miséricorde had joined forces to become one order now called Les Soeurs de Marie Joseph et de la Miséricorde. I could not prevent myself from feeling giddy when I learned that Reverend Mother from Bordeaux was now in their retirement convent in Auteuil.

My host took me on a tour of the Novitiate. Due to a falling off in vocations, it was now forlorn and empty of any signs of being occupied. In spite of it being a warm and sunny day, a cold shiver ran up and down my spine. Sister Jeremiah explained that some of the elderly Sisters now occupied the upper floors, where I had spent my time as a novice. A lift had been installed at the bottom of the stairs. The big brass ball still adorned the bannister. What struck me most were the changes to the grounds and gardens. Gone were the neatly trimmed box hedge borders and gravel walkways. The fruit trees and vegetable patches had been replaced by grass and the odd weed here and there. I chuckled to myself, remembering the penance I had to do for my escapade on the bicycle. She was interested in how I had coped after I left the convent. Things were going nicely until I started to inquire about some of the sisters I had known and worked with. At this point, I mentioned my angel, Breda. I was told that she had died. She began to tell me so and so had died or retired, and I started to cry. A great sadness came upon me suddenly. I could not control it. A tightness gripped me, and my throat became so narrow that I could hardly breathe. While retreating to the door leading out onto the street, I heard her saying that I would be welcome to join the nuns in their chapel for Mass the following day.

Outside in the street, I tried desperately to compose myself. Sitting down on a low wall, I let the tears flow. It was then I realised that I had, in fact, given some of the best years of my youth to the service of the Congregation and had received very little in return. Had those years been wasted? Has my life been a series of failures? Had I made a mistake in entering religious life as a naive 17-year-old? These questions had haunted me like ghosts in the innermost chambers of my heart and soul for years. Were the trials and tribulations I had subsequently endured punishment from God for my sins and weaknesses? My mind in turmoil, and with these thoughts swirling around and around in my head, I arrived at the auberge teary-eyed and weary. My hosts asked me if I would require dinner and offered me a cold drink. I later retired to my room, feeling restored in mind and body. I began to count my blessings.

The next morning, after a good night's sleep, I returned to the convent for morning Mass. In the chapel, I gazed at the walls, the high ceiling. I thanked God for my health and my two children, for my independence and most of all, for the freedom I now enjoyed. I would never regret having delved into religious life. It had been a positive experience; I had learned the language of the country, I had met and worked with some great people and had visited many interesting places.

The experiences and skills I had acquired had left a lasting legacy. It was time for me to move away from any negative thoughts of the past. In spite of this newfound positivity, fear of a judgmental God, feelings of low self-esteem and failure persisted in my innermost consciousness. The humility into which I had been indoctrinated during my years in religious life still lingered and had somehow become twisted into a lack of self-worth, a reluctance to defend myself when criticised or put down, and an acceptance of misplaced authority. In other words, I lacked autonomy. These shortcomings were to stay with me for many years, causing untold stress and anxiety. The long journey to recovery lay ahead. There were many mountains to climb before my soul would feel free.

Leaving the lovely little French town in the province of Haute-Vienne, I felt buoyed in the knowledge that I had done the right thing in revisiting the place where I had spent some of the happiest days of my youth. It was the place where I had been closest to the Lord, where I had prayed, had served God, albeit for a short time, and had learned lessons that would be useful for the rest of my entire life, such as the virtue of waste not, want not and prioritising tasks in order of importance. Materialism or worldly possessions have never been important to me. I learned to respect people of other religions, those more unfortunate, and those in need.

Epilogue

HAVING RETIRED FROM MY EMPLOYMENT with Balbriggan Area Project Association, empty nest syndrome began to creep up on me. My two daughters had left home: Catherine to live in her own apartment in Drogheda, and Joanne had taken off on her OE to Australia and New Zealand. In 2007 I decided to visit Joanne, where she was working as a journalist in Westport, New Zealand. My holiday visa would last three months. I packed my bags and bought my airline ticket. I was very excited about seeing a new faraway country I knew very little about. All I knew was that it was further away than Australia, that rugby was their game, and that, unlike Australia, it sometimes snowed. This was about all I had heard of this land. In spite of looking forward to my trip, I was very apprehensive about the long journey, which meant flying Aer Lingus to London and getting connecting Singapore Airlines flights to Auckland via Singapore. Arriving totally jet-lagged in Auckland, I was happy that I had pre-booked two nights in Auckland, where I slept continuously for two days.

The two Air New Zealand flights to Wellington and Westport went well until we reached the West Coast of the South Island. Wind and rain caused the small plane to shake violently. It felt like ages hovering over the edge of the sea. The enormous waves were getting closer. Panic gripped me as the plane was descending. I could not see an airport. As the wheels were being lowered, I closed my eyes. When I opened them again, we were taxiing on the small runway. A member of the crew welcomed us to Westport. I could not believe I was actually there. The airport building consisted of a little wooden structure surrounded by a few parked cars. After a very joyful reunion with my daughter, while making our way on the short car journey to the hotel in the town, she pointed out Carters Beach. Crossing the big bridge spanning the Buller River, I was awestruck by the scenery. The lush vegetation made me realise that I had arrived in a country rich in conservation and unspoiled views. We rented a house in Bright Street. Before long, I had a bike to take me shopping and sightseeing. The beach attracted me like a magnet. On long walks, I was amazed at the wild beauty of the totally unspoiled landscape. The snow-covered mountain peaks were visible from where we lived, and the sunsets were stunning. I was so enthralled by the West Coast that I applied to extend my visitor's visa by five months. When my eldest daughter Catherine, who had been travelling in Asia, joined us at Christmas of that year, I was more than happy. Visits to the blowholes in Punakaiki left me speechless. The temperate climate suited me. Time flies when we are enjoying ourselves, and when the time came for me to say goodbye to New Zealand, I felt that my absence would be very short. I was determined to return as soon as possible.

Back in Balbriggan, I became the proud grandmother of my first grandchild. Katelyn was born in Our Lady of Lourdes hospital in Drogheda on 30th December 2008. Unfortunately, due to immigration complications, her New Zealand father could not remain in Ireland. When the baby was three months old, her parents took her to New Zealand. This was heartbreaking for me, and I returned to Invercargill for another three months. This became a pattern of travelling between

Ireland and New Zealand until I decided to apply for and was granted a Resident Visa on 19th November 2013. This was for five years, during which time I was the happiest new immigrant in New Zealand, and my joy increased with the arrival of my grandson, Johnny Mac.

Those first years of toing and froing between New Zealand and Ireland made me wish that I could be in two places at the same time. While in New Zealand, I missed my sisters and brothers, their children and their grandchildren. Being part of a large family in Ireland meant that life was one continual party – wedding, baptisms, birthdays, Christmas, St Patrick's Day and Easter. But being near my daughters and grandchildren won the day!

The excitement of travelling to Ireland and Balbriggan starts as soon as I book my ticket. This is usually many months beforehand. Oh, the joy of seeing my four sisters and two brothers again. With each of us having children and grandchildren, the special occasions are numerous, the inevitable funeral also being cause for a gathering of the clan. We are all getting older, and these reunions are lively and joyful. I also look forward to seeing friends again. It's hard to express in words the feeling one gets when stepping onto Irish soil. Although tired and jet-lagged, the whiff of air at Dublin Airport is enough to give new life to the soul and to invigorate a wretched body.

Balbriggan has changed in many ways down through the years. It has greatly expanded geographically. New housing estates have sprung up to accommodate the rising population. At the 2016 census, the population had risen to 21,722 from a paltry 8000 back in my childhood. This in no way diminishes the friendly atmosphere that still prevails. Heavy traffic that once passed through the main street has now been diverted through a by-pass ring road constructed during improved infrastructure. In order to cater for the inflated population, there are now ten primary and five secondary schools. Many clubs provide recreation and sport. Mill Street's new cinema has replaced the old Savoy, which is now the Combined Clubs Community Centre in Dublin Street. To the east of the railway, the harbour and beaches have not changed, except that the diving board at the Black Rock has gone. The lighthouse and Martello tower still remind us of times past, and the Sailor's Grave now has a plaque, which was placed there by the local Historical Society. The Parish Church of St Peter and Paul has been upgraded and maintained impeccably. Together with St George's Church of Ireland, many other denominational churches now exist in the town. The Bracken Court Hotel graces the town square beside a new public library and Council offices. The town is surrounded by new industrial enterprises, providing employment and training. A new shopping complex at Millfield adds convenience and vibrancy to the area.

Travelling from one end of New Zealand to the other to visit each of my daughters is a way of discovering the geography of the two largest islands. In every city or town, I am amazed at the visual difference between these places and Irish towns. I'm struck by the slower pace of life and, most of all, by the people. Māori culture was a new discovery for me. The Marae in Bluff was my first introduction to the artistic heritage of these people. It is their meeting place, their cultural mecca where they conduct funerals and celebrate joyful occasions. Living in a rented house in Bluff for a year allowed me to enjoy being at the most southern large port in New Zealand and the last port of call for ships heading to Antarctica. The views from Bluff Hill are extraordinary, and I enjoyed my time there immensely. From there, I spent some time in Invercargill to be near Catherine and Ross and my grandchildren.

When the opportunity to come back to the West Coast of the South Island presented itself, I did not hesitate to return to where I had first landed in New Zealand. I had previously been to Greymouth, and when my daughter went to work there, I decided that I would rent a small place and see how things progressed. She and her husband Mark had a little girl called Maira, and the family settled in Nelson Street. As months and years went by, I settled into the town and made friends. The birth of their second child Roisin gave me added joy and reason to remain on the West Coast. I am absolutely overawed by the scenery, be it the beaches, the bush or the view of the Ranges. The town lies in the centre of the coast, and whether one heads north, south or inland, I constantly count my lucky stars to be in such wonderful surroundings.

During the whitebait season, people line the riverbanks catching enormous amounts of tiny transparent, matchstick-sized fish in fine-mesh nets. When prepared and cooked with flour and beaten eggs, they taste delicious. Divers prise paua (the Māori term for abalone shellfish) from underwater rocks and scoop out the black flesh to make patties.

Mutton birds are another speciality. Found mainly on the islands off the south coast at Bluff, the chicks are deemed more tender, the preparation of which is a lengthy process. Plucked and cleaned, they are then immersed in cold water and boiled three times in order to remove the excess fat. They make a tasty morsel but are a little too salty for me.

Whenever I visit Auckland on my way to Ireland, it was and still is one of my favourite places. The beaches are safe and well maintained. Taking the short ferry ride from the harbour to Devonport invariably takes my breath away. Visiting the Naval Museum is interesting, and I love the atmosphere of the outdoor cafés and restaurants.

Christchurch, too, has always been a joy to visit. The journey there, passing through the Buller Gorge when I lived in Westport, never failed to amaze me.

When Christchurch was shattered by the 6.3 earthquake on 22nd February 2011, I had just left there two days previously to go to Westport. I was due to fly out from there to Wellington at 5 pm on the 22nd. Arriving at the airport in Westport, I was informed that all flights had been cancelled. Well, there I was, stranded with nowhere to stay and not knowing how or when I would be able to leave. I need not have worried; friends who we had made years ago offered me dinner and a bed for the night. Not only did they look after me, but they also arranged transport for me to go the following day to Nelson in a freight truck, and from there, a flight would take me over the Cook Strait to Wellington. Such is the hospitality and kindness of the people of the West Coast.

Now back living on the West Coast of beautiful New Zealand, I am writing at this time for my four grandchildren. With the exception of my 12-year-old granddaughter, who was born in Ireland, the three others are Kiwis. I want them to know about their Irish grandmother and grandfather and their Irish relations back in Balbriggan and Rush, County Dublin.

Although I miss my family in Ireland, my New Zealand family wins, hands down. My visits to Balbriggan are always looked forward to with great excitement, but I could not envisage living too far away from my grandchildren.

Taking one day at a time, I realise that faith, hope and charity are the virtues I strive to practice most. Faith is the most difficult. At a time when God appears to be absent in our everyday lives, materialism takes over far too often. Exposure to religion has diminished greatly, and as my practice has become limited, I am guilty of imploring His help only when catastrophe occurs, instead of giving thanks for what I already have. Hope, on the other hand, is what I tend to rely on. I hope that God really does exist, that He is a loving and caring entity, that death is not the end, and that our efforts in this life will not have been in vain. All this and more are what I hope for. Charity is not always easy when we are faced with difficult events and people. As the bible tells us, "Love thy neighbour as thyself". In an age when love has been misrepresented by images and stories, I like to think that I have been greatly blessed in my life by tremendous real love and affection. From the day that I was born, I have been surrounded with love by my parents, family and friends, and for this, I am truly grateful.

THE END

AUTHOR'S NOTE

The stories in this book are all true and based on my memories but some names have been changed to protect identities.

Endeavouring to recount events within the social, religious and cultural mores of the early and mid-20th century, some historical items that have greatly influenced the ebb and flow of growing up in post-WWII Ireland have been included. Also included are accounts of my mother's two brothers who fought in WWI and the Irish Civil War of Independence, respectively: Paddy Hoey with the British Army in Ypres and Thomas with the Irish Republican Army. These stories nurtured me in a non-judgemental and open-minded environment, and so it is important to me that they be mentioned here. They are, after all, a part of the stories I am leaving to nourish my grandchildren's family history.

ACKNOWLEDGEMENTS

I would like to express my sincere gratitude to everyone who helped me in the writing of this memoir. Authors Paddy Richardson, Wendy Scott and Paul Maunder for their invaluable feedback and guidance. To CopyPress for putting it all together with style. Special thanks to Martin McNamara for the magnificent cover photograph of Balbriggan lighthouse, chosen for the childhood memories it envokes. The Mawhera Writers group for ongoing support and encouragement especially Katrina Brown and Mary Prendergast who have been wonderful friends throughout the process. My neighbour Chrissie Hampton for her help and encouragement. Sorcha O'Malley of Detail Proofreading & Editing whose professionalism was second to none. To my daughter Joanne Naish whose support and editing was much appreciated. And lastly to my family in Ireland, whose unwavering support, love and humour, have greatly influenced this book.

WANTAGE, FARINGDON
& THE VALE VILLAGES
IN OLD PHOTOGRAPHS

THIS FAMOUS VIEW ACROSS THE VALE illustrates the advantage of the position of the nearby hillfort. The White Horse lies above his Manger, overlooking Dragon Hill, where St George slew the dragon. The spilled blood prevents grass growing on the spot, so goes the legend – one of many associated with the area. In fact, Dragon Hill was artificially levelled sometime in the past.

WANTAGE, FARINGDON
& THE VALE VILLAGES
IN OLD PHOTOGRAPHS

COLLECTED BY
NANCY HOOD

ALAN SUTTON
1987

Alan Sutton Publishing Limited
Brunswick Road · Gloucester

First published 1987

British Library Cataloguing in Publication Data

Wantage and Faringdon in old photographs.
1. Faringdon Region (Oxfordshire)—History
—Pictorial works   2. Wantage Region
(Oxfordshire)—History—Pictorial works
3. Faringdon Region (Oxfordshire)—
Description and travel—Views 4. Wantage
Region (Oxfordshire)—Description and
travel—Views
I. Hood, Nancy
942.5'76   DA690.F227

ISBN 0-86299-458-6

Cover: THE MAYO BROTHERS' SMITHY was behind the Shears, Mill Street, and also in Grove Street, Wantage.

Typesetting and origination by
Alan Sutton Publishing Limited
Printed in Great Britain
by WBC Print Limited · Bristol

CONTENTS

THE LOYD LINDSAYS of the Lockinge Estate were the largest landowners in Berkshire. Lord Wantage was an MP and High Sheriff, playing an active role in both national politics and local affairs. Here the Provincial Grand Lodge of Berkshire Freemasons meet at Lockinge House, July 1900.

INTRODUCTION

A traveller's view of this western part of the Vale of the White Horse is not so very different from that of John Leland, in the reign of Elizabeth I: from Oxford he found 'The ground was meatly wooddy ... thens 10 mils al by chaumpain and sum corne, but most pasture to Faringdon.' Towards Wantage by Hanney there was 'hilly ground well wooddid and fruitefull of corne ... by lovelle ground in sum partes marschy ... unto Wanetinge that standithe on the right ripe (bank) of a praty broke ...'

Both Wantage and Faringdon still lie in a predominantly agricultural landscape – a scene in which the details change while the overall impression is one of continuity. Where Leland noticed open field, woodland, pasture and low marshy ground, improvements in machinery, drainage and fertilisers in the last two hundred years have enabled more land to be turned to arable fields.

Some of this change has been recorded by the Victorian country photographer – but his camera takes us back only a little over a hundred years. Not until after 1910 did local newspapers use photographs extensively to enliven their columns of small print and adverts. The Kodak Brownie did much to fill the gap, early in this century, in family portraits, souvenir photographs and snapshots taken for the pure novelty of it. Through these photographs we can relate to the lives of the ordinary people who lived in our locality just before us, and see the changes in the town and countryside around them.

The chances are that, in a village of 500–700 people, a hundred years ago, everyone was working within a mile of so of his home. Settlement in the Vale of the White Horse developed in close relationship to the geology and structure of the clay vale and chalk and limestone hills. The Oxford clay of the Thames Valley, the limestone North Berks Ridge, the clays of the Vale proper, the greensand and chalk steps up the steep scarp slope, lie in broad bands running east–west. Each type of clay, sand and stone yields a characteristic soil which in turn determines what can be best grown, grazed or built on it.

Early man cleared the birch and pine woodlands of the chalk downs because his tools of stone and bone could tackle it; the first fields, the remains of which can still be seen at Knighton and Letcombe Downs, were on chalk. The oldest monument made by man in the area, Wayland's Smithy long barrow, was built on a pavement of sarsen stones cleared for fields over 5000 years ago. Later, iron tools enabled the heavier oak forest on the clay soils to be cleared and managed as coppices, fields and meadow.

Settlement then moved from the downs to the spring-line, formed where rain water soaking through the chalk hit marl or clay and burst to the surface. The spring-line, already followed by a lowland summer-road parallel to the Ridgeway, was settled at least by Roman times. Remains of villas or farmsteads have been found at Woolstone, Uffington, Baulking, Fawler, Challow, Stanford, Letcombe and Wantage, under the chalk scarp, and similarly on the northern limestone ridge from Faringdon to Cumnor. These villa estates would have had pasture on the uplands, spring water, meadow along the brooks and a loamy sandy soil in between for arable fields.

This pattern was taken over by Saxon settlers and these estates are some of the first to be recorded historically. The charters of the ninth century, which listed the boundaries of a property when it changed hands, survive for almost the whole of the Vale; in them are recorded the roots of the parish and village of today. The long strips of land, running at right angles to the ridges, have become known as 'strip parishes'. Their shape was determined by the need for a variety of soils for viable settlement: meadow for cows, land near the village for cornfields, orchards, a water supply, and upland pasture for sheep.

Markets developed around some of these manorial estates – the gift of the king as at Wantage, or the privilege of an abbey, as at Shellingford. The tolls and dues might make the fortunes of the local lord and the rights to fairs and markets were the source of many disputes. In 1276, a 50-year tussle between Fulk Fitzwaryn of Wantage and the Abbot of Abingdon over competing fairs resulted in the killing by Fulk's men of one Seman of Shellingford and strong-arm tactics to force the fair-goers to Wantage. Other medieval markets were at Shrivenham, Faringdon, Stanford, Baulking and East Hendred. There, in addition, two yearly cloth fairs stretched up the 'Golden Mile' from the village up the downs. The village feast on the saint's day of the dedication of the parish church is often a relic of these fairs.

By chance Wantage and Faringdon have been the survivors as market towns. Leland said that Faringdon, known as Cheping, or Market Faringdon, now had 'none or very small market' at that time. But at Faringdon there was an attempt to organise the growing town as a Borough by the thirteenth century – there were 51 long narrow burgage plots laid out along what is now London Road, and the medieval South Street, High Street, Gildon Street and Claypits. Those along London Road remain in the modern property boundaries, and together with the Market Place, Cornmarket and church, mark the heart of the medieval town.

The market was the focus of Wantage too, across the brook from the presumed centre of Roman occupation, near the parish church. The town remained a collection of four manors struggling under the administrative institutions of the feudal system, until the rights of the Lords of the Manor were finally purchased by the Town Commissioners in 1868. Some of the medieval closes leading from the Market Place survive in Wantage, where the encroachment of groups of shops on to the wide open Market Square is evident.

The two towns have contrasting buildings too: Faringdon's stone façades are said to be copies of the style of Coleshill House built c. 1650–62 for Sir George Pratt to designs by Inigo Jones. Otherwise it is honey-coloured ashlar or rubblestone quarried nearby, with stone tile roofs. Brick works, established in the mid-eighteenth century wherever clay and sand were conveniently to hand, provided materials for the modest expansion along the turnpike roads leading from the town.

Use of bricks can be seen more dramatically in Wantage, where the half-timbered gables of the Market Place were re-fronted immediately the new building material became available. Brickworks were at Uffington, Fernham, Faringdon, Eaton Hastings, Stanford, Childrey and even at Lockinge, on the downs.

With coal coming by canal (1810), and soon afterwards by rail (1840), brickmaking and other industries serving the farming villages around, such as agricultural engineering, milling, malting and brewing, took off. The countryside must have hummed with the noise of steam engines. Back in the villages the steam age did not empty the land for the towns as in the industrial north; populations doubled over the nineteenth century.

Farming, dairying and woodland management, or one of the many crafts and skills which supported the farmer, continued to provide employment. Blacksmiths, carpenters, wheelwrights, millers, thatchers, masons, shoemakers, tailors, bakers, publicans might all be found in a medium-sized village. Boys went to work in the fields, or perhaps took an apprenticeship which kept them out of trouble in virtually indentured labour for seven years; girls went into domestic service. The pattern changed not so much with steam and the Great War, as with the motor car engine and then the Second World War.

The second half of this century has seen the development of the towns and villages taken in hand by planners. It is the link between the people and the land that has been broken: the companies on the industrial estates do not necessarily relate to the products of the countryside and not so many people live and work in the same community. It is harder to keep the community working together. A look back through these old photographs, which document some of these changes up to 1974, may bring the past back into focus.

Nancy Hood
August 1987

SOUVENIR OF COLESHILL

THE WINDMILL

OF

THE CHURCH

SOUVENIR

COLESHILL

A BIT OF COLESHILL

VILLAGE LOOKING NORTH

THE SCHOOLS

NO ONE HAS REGRETTED THE LOSS OF THIS UGLY TOWN HALL, which lasted only 50 years before being removed to make way for the statue of Alfred the Great in 1877.

THE TOWN HALL which replaced it can be seen beyond the statue – a mock-Tudor style building occasionally said to be by G.E. Street, but this is doubtful.

The Market, Wantage.

THE SOUTH SIDE OF WANTAGE MARKET PLACE still has the Georgian façades, seen here in 1911.

ARBERY'S has hardly changed; here it is decorated for the Jubilee of 1935 – note the portraits of King George V and Queen Mary.

SHOPS MOVED PREMISES OFTEN — Belcher's moved from here on Church Lane to a site next to the Post Office. The last Belcher retired in 1983.

ONE OF THE OLDEST IRONMONGERS IN WANTAGE, Kent's shop is decorated for Queen Victoria's Jubilee in 1887.

ESTABLISHED OVER A CENTURY.

Messrs. J. E. & F. Cottrell

Purveyors of the finest quality
⌀ BEEF and MUTTON. ⌀

The Oldest Butchers' Establishment in the Town.

Specialities : { PRIME   CALVES HEADS,
                 PICKLED   SWEETBREADS,
                 TONGUES.   CORNED BEEF.

All Orders by Post will receive prompt attention.

❦ ❦ ❦

Market Place, WANTAGE. Telephone No. 7.

THIS HALF-TIMBERED JETTIED SHOP was taken down in the 1950s, the beginning of the end for the north side of Wantage Market Place.

KATE EVANS AND EVE HARRIS stand outside their shop on Wantage Market Place, c. 1920.

WANTAGE STORES, c. 1926, was a single episode in 300 years of a grocer's business on this Market Place property.

THREE GENERATIONS OF HUGHES kept a shoemaker's shop in Wantage. Sidney Hughes, here with his sister in front of the shop on the Market Place, c. 1935, retired in the 1960s.

THE CHANGE TO READY-TO-WEAR SUPPLIERS had advantages with slick advertising.

BEHIND THE GEORGIAN FAÇADE lie gabled half-timbered buildings, some 300 years old. This was the former Crown of Old England, a coaching inn – note the covered carriageway.

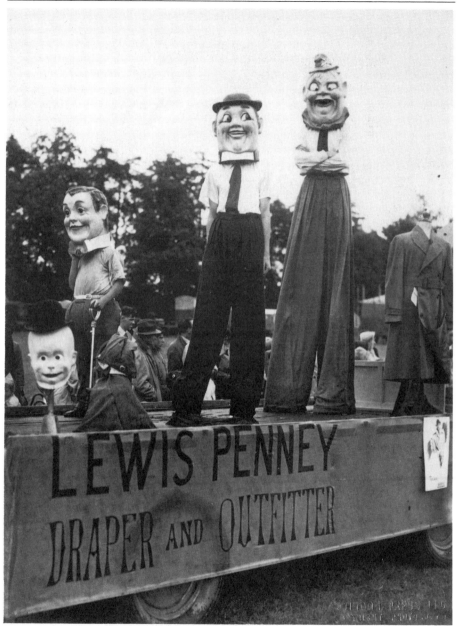

LEWIS PENNEY'S FLOAT at the 1954 Carnival advertises in a cheerful post-war atmosphere.

BREWERS AND MALTSTERS,
Wine and Spirit Merchants,
— WANTAGE. —

WINES OF EXCELLENT QUALITY AND 'SPECIAL' SPIRITS.
PRICE LIST.

	Per. Gall.		Per. Doz.
BOOTH'S GIN	14 0	...	28 0
OLD JAMAICA RUM	16 0	...	32 0
FINE COGNAC BRANDY, Pale & Brown	28 0	...	56 0
OLD IRISH WHISKY	18 0	...	36 0
OLD SCOTCH WHISKY ...	18 0	...	36 0
BRITISH BRANDY, Pale & Brown ...	16 0	...	32 0
PORTS, Fine Old and Tawny ... From	24 0	to	48 0
SHERRIES, Fine Old Pale and Brown ,,	24 0	to	48 0
CLARETS, ... ,,	12 0	to	24 0
BURGUNDIES ... ... ,,	24 0	to	36 0

(FINE COGNAC BRANDY, OLD IRISH WHISKY, OLD SCOTCH WHISKY — Guaranteed 6 Years Old.)

CHAMPAGNE, all leading Brands at current prices.

DITTO, 'Vin d' Ay,' dry sparkling, 2/6, pint ; 4/6, quart.

LIQUEURS : Cherry Brandy, Sloe Gin, Ginger Brandy, Ginger Gin, Orange Bitters, Peppermint, Cloves, &c.

ALL GOODS DELIVERED FREE.
☞ FOR BEER PRICE LIST SEE OVER.

MARKET PLACE in 1895, with the Portwell given to the town in the sixteenth century by Sir Henry Unton.

MARKET PLACE, Faringdon, 1930s.

STAFF PHOTOGRAPHS were taken of Chamberlain's Grocers, Market Place, Faringdon, in 1909 and 1931.

FARINGDON'S SHEEP MARKET was in Market Place and the cattle market was on Church Street.

AT THE OTHER END OF FARINGDON'S HIGH STREET from the Market Place was the Corn Exchange, built in 1863.

THESE TWO VIEWS OF FARINGDON'S TOWN CENTRE show the seventeenth-century Market House before (1901) and after (1905) it began to be used as the Fire Station. The Crown, to the right, is of Elizabethan date, although it has been re-fronted many times.

ON LONDON STREET the closely packed shops reflect the medieval property boundaries, seen here in 1904 (above) and the 1930s (below).

HENRY ROBINS AND EDGAR ARGANT are in front of Ann's Garage, Marlborough Street, Faringdon, 1912.

MARLBOROUGH STREET is seen here in the 1930s.

OUTSIDE PARKER'S REFRESHMENT ROOMS, also Corn Stores, Baker and Confectioner on Marlborough Street, Faringdon, stand left to right: Mr Edington, Horace Hickman, J. Parker and Frank Wheeler in 1916.

GLOUCESTER STREET, Faringdon, 1895.

GRAVEL WALK, Faringdon, 1905.

Cross Roads, Faringdon.

THIS CROSSROADS IN FARINGDON is now almost unrecognisable as a busy roundabout, c. 1910.

Church Lane, Ashbury.

FROM CHURCH LANE, Ashbury, there is a view across the Vale of the White Horse.

SHRIVENHAM'S WIDE MAIN STREET was always a busy turnpike road, but who in the 30s would think it might need a by pass?

KENT'S ROW, GROVE, was owned by Kents, the Ironmongers, of Wantage. The thatched half was once a yeoman farm house, first extended, then divided into five cottages. Outside, on Main Street, stands Edgar Povey, who worked for the Railway, c. 1910. The cottages have now gone.

THE WHITE HORSE PUB, at Woolstone, is one of several in the area named after the chalk horse on the downs.

A PENNY STAMP sent this postcard from Kingston Lisle, showing the village shop and Post Office in 1919.

BUCKLAND'S STONE WALLS AND THATCHED COTTAGES are built with the coral ragstone of the North Berkshire Ridge.

THIS STONE-WALLED ROSE GARDEN is in Longworth.

STANFORD-IN-THE-VALE had three village greens; this is Church Green.

THERE IS A LONG VILLAGE STREET — note here the sun reflecting on the blue and red brickwork.

THE VILLAGE OF LETCOMBE BASSETT has a classic situation at the foot of the Downs, on the spring-line.

SELDOM WERE PEOPLE ABOUT IN THE VILLAGES; in Letcombe Regis here the trap and the haycart meet.

THE PLOUGH AT EAST HANNEY is now the Vintage Restaurant.

VILLAGERS STAND AROUND THE LITTLE GREEN at the crossroads, East Hanney, c. 1900 – a less than quiet spot today.

THE GREEN AT CHILDREY was the centre of village life – the pub, the Hatchet, was on the right, the pond in the centre and the wheelwright's on the left, c. 1899.

AN IRON BRIDGE crosses the Ock River at East Hanney.

WALLS MADE OF COB AND THATCH were once common in villages without a local supply of stone – a few survive at East Hendred.

ALL OF THE THATCHED ROOFS HAVE DISAPPEARED from this corner of Horn Lane and the road to the Downs at East Hendred.

THIS VIEW OF THE SQUARE, WATCHFIELD, is dated 1908 by the postmark.

AT CHILDREY, The Crown pub greeted the traveller along the hollow-way leading from the Downs.

AT THE VILLAGE PUMP, Letcombe Regis, is Alice Alder, standing with some of the village children; Louise Addis and Lil Wilmot sit together on the second step. 1904/5.

THE BAKER'S ARMS was on Uffington High Street, with Chapel Lane leading off, 1916.

GEESE STRUT ACROSS THE GOOSE GREEN at Goosey, in a scene which could be 200 years ago.

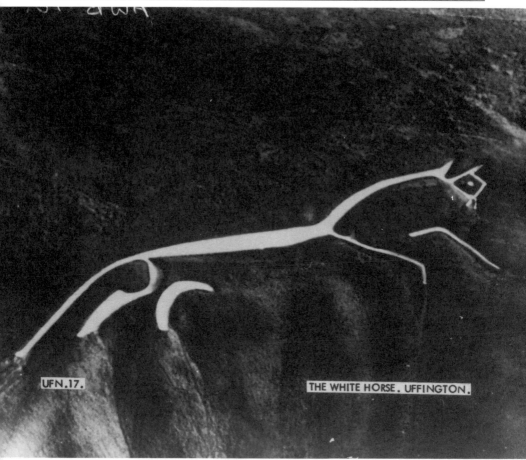

UFN.17.

THE WHITE HORSE. UFFINGTON.

CAN YOU SEE ANOTHER WHITE HORSE? Has it always been this shape? Some would say that erosion has changed the position of the legs and the width of the body. The Uffington horse is the oldest of all the white horses carved into the chalk, and probably dates from the late Iron Age.

WAYLAND'S SMITHY LONG BARROW truly resembled a cave in its tumbled-down state, prior to reconstruction in the 1960s. Legend has associated it with the gods and heroes of the Germanic homeland of the Anglo-Saxons – the angry smith who hurled stones at people and who worked at night. The tale of Weland the Smith is a bloodthirsty one of imprisonment, lust, murder and revenge.

RIGHT:
THE TOMB WAS EXCAVATED in 1962/3 and the great sarsen stones replaced upright; here a later ditch across the forecourt is being examined. Four of the original sarsen stones survived intact; the tallest is ten feet high and weighs four tons. Excavation determined its true function as a burial monument – in fact two barrows existed in the mound, each containing burials nearly 5000 years old.

Blowing Stone, Uffington

THE BLOWING STONE is in a former pub garden at Kingston Lisle. Children still try to re-create Alfred's trumpeting of victory over the Danes at Ashdown by blowing through the fossil root holes.

MATTHEW ARNOLD'S FYFIELD ELM was featured in his poem 'The Scholar Gipsy', written while at Oxford. It has since been felled.

MISS SIMMONDS stands by the isolated Pitchpoles Well at Letcombe, in a scene which shows the scrub woodland cover on the Downs before they came almost completely under the plough.

GREAT COXWELL TITHE BARN has always been a favourite subject for country photographer's rural scenes. This one was from Antonia of Swindon and Devizes. The barn, of Cotswold stone with a stone tile roof, dates from the thirteenth century and once held the produce of the grange farms of Beaulieu Abbey.

The Tower. Faringdon Folly

FARINGDON FOLLY, built by Lord Berner in 1935, is perhaps the last great folly built in England. It is 140 feet high and may be on the site of the twelfth-century fortifications of Stephen and Matilda.

THIS WING OF CHARNEY BASSETT MANOR is the solar and undercroft of a Norman manor house, once a grange farm of Abingdon Abbey. It is one of the best in the region, and dates from the thirteenth century.

FARINGDON HOUSE was built by Sir Henry Pye, Poet Laureate, 1780–5, and replaced an earlier enormous gabled manor.

KING'S MANOR, East Hendred, was one of five in this wealthy cloth-producing medieval village. Opposite stood the Pound, with stocks and pillory, and a small chantry chapel, now known as Champs Chapel.

A TRAGIC FIRE destroyed Coleshill House in 1952. It was thought to be the best Inigo Jones-inspired house of the mid seventeenth century in England, with a splendid staircase and plaster ceilings.

ASHDOWN HOUSE, built of chalk, was a rural escape from the plague for the first Earl of Craven, c. 1660. Much of its former surrounding forest with radiating avenues has gone, revealing the sarsen stones, 'grey wethers', in the park.

STYLES COTTAGE, Upper Common, Uffington, is really two cottages – the left side was built in the seventeenth century and the right side added later. In 1861 two farm labourers' families lived there, one with six children, one with nine; there are three rooms upstairs. It belonged to the Craven Estate.

THOMAS AND EMILY HERBERT stand in front of their Lockinge Estate cottage (c. 1930), a substantial seventeenth-century one which was not pulled down by the Loyd-Lindsays during their re-housing of the estate workers in the 1860s.

BEHIND THIS CHALK AND BRICK COTTAGE AT UFFINGTON can be seen the old fire station, 1916.

THIS TINY COTTAGE on a triangular piece of waste, Sheephouse Fields Cottage, with its pig-sty and chicken run, used to house agricultural labourers of the Longworth Estate. Later a family of hawkers lived there and called it 'Abingdon Villa'.

THESE MODEL ESTATE HOUSES belong to the Pusey Estate, and are almost adjacent to the House, Park and church.

G.E. STREET designed this gothic-style estate housing at Charney Bassett in 1852 – a small scale model village for the Pusey Estate.

THESE COTTAGES IN HANNEY AND SPARSHOLT, condemned in the 1960s, show what dark and crowded lives lay behind our view of life in the country.

THIS TERRACE WAS BUILT FOR THE CANAL WHARF AT GROVE, which lay on the other side. They have been virtually rebuilt, but left to right, they are Wharf Cottage, the Carpenter's, the Boatman's, the Stable and Blacksmith's.

NEW HOUSING AT GROVE illustrates the pressure on the villages which comes with new jobs on the industrial estates and research centres in the market towns. Once a hamlet, Grove now approaches Wantage in population. So far though, amenities have not kept pace.

HORSE-DRAWN PLOUGHS sit in the field below the manger, overlooked by the White Horse.

THE COUNTRY PHOTOGRAPHER has found an obliging real white horse in the Vale.

NOTE THE VARIETY OF MEADOW FLOWERS IN THE HAYFIELD at Letcombe. Everyone turned out for the hay harvest, but now it is mowed quickly by tractor.

ON THE HORSE-DRAWN REAPER BINDER at West Hendred, are Bill Seares, Fred Roberts and his mother Patty Roberts, 1920–30.

THE STEAM ENGINE here at Wier Farm, East Hanney, came from Dandridge's Mill, 1900–1910. Bobby Ford is threshing with the Eadys on their farm.

THE COMBINE HARVESTER, seen here at Fernham, needs but one operator.

VALE FARMS were formerly mainly dairy farms – famous for cheeses in the shape of hares and pineapples, and of a single-Gloucester type. Milk production replaced butter and cheesemaking in the nineteenth century, when it could easily be sent by train. Here cows still graze upon Grove Green, 1910.

SHEEP ARE PASTURED ON THE DOWNS ABOVE LETCOMBE; the water barrel is an improvement over the dew pond.

G. TYLER was shepherd at Letcombe. The sheep are of a Down variety, less common today.

RADCOT BRIDGE was one of the traditional sheep-washing places along the river – this scene was in 1885.

MR HERBERT, whose cottage appears on p.61, surveys a field of giant mangels at Lockinge, around 1900. These were introduced into England in the early eighteenth century to improve winter fodder for sheep.

DOUGLAS EADY, aged 10, whose father also worked on the Estate, was caught by the photographer in the same field at Lockinge.

A FAMILY SNAPSHOT is taken while the hay rick is being thatched, c. 1930, at Lockinge.

A PHOTOGRAPH ALBUM from Letcombe Regis manor is unusual in having many snapshots of the farm labourers. Here are A. Morris and E. Francis outside the house, and Mr S. Kent with the shire-horses, opposite.

R8/78/25

BEEHIVES IN THE KITCHEN GARDEN at Letcombe ensure pollination of the fruit trees as well as a honey supply.

IN CHILDREY the Smiths owned the traction engine to be hired out to farmers, left to right: Arthur Smith junior, Arthur Smith senior, Frank Edmonds (driver), a carpenter, Jim Preston, Mr Preston senior, boy from Little (West) Challow.

MR W. STONE, blacksmith, hammers a horseshoe at the Harrison's Forge at East Hendred, 1926. This village, like many, had several smithies to deal with the making and repair of agricultural implements as well as shoeing horses.

HARRISON'S ABANDONED FORGE AND WHEELWRIGHT'S SHOP is the consequence of the change from horse-drawn wagons and equipment to tractors. The tyring kiln and huge sarsen stone tyring ring are still there, all waiting to be turned into a village museum.

NALDER AND NALDER ENGINEERING COMPANY at East Challow employed around 200 men at the turn of the century. The business began by making ploughs, threshing machines and portable steam engines for the local market, but added sieving and grading machines for malt, cocoa and coffee beans, which were shipped all over the Empire. Their malt-grading machines can still be seen in remote distilleries in Scotland.

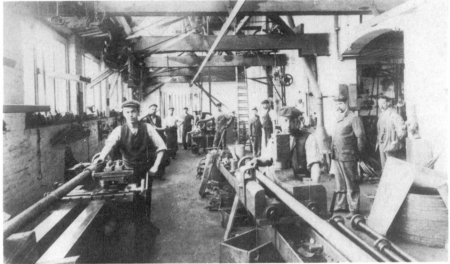

APPRENTICESHIPS WERE FOR SEVEN YEARS. During the war, local women worked there on munitions and some found they preferred the work to domestic service. But the jobs went back to the lads afterwards.

THE BRICKWORKS AT BOW, Stanford-in-the-Vale, used sand and clay dug on the site, but there is nothing left of these works today.

THE BRICKWORKS AT UFFINGTON supplied bricks for repairing labourers' cottages and a spate of speculative building on the fringes of Faringdon and Wantage. This engine house survived for agricultural use after the works closed between the wars.

SWAN LANE, FARINGDON, home of Westall's Bakery – the ovens are still there. Photographed in 1979.

BILL LAY'S VILLAGE BAKERY at East Hanney was still going strong in the 1930s. Rose Cross holds the cottage loaf with Fred Carr in the hat; Mr Lay is on the right.

THE BAKER OF WEST HENDRED, F.H. Goodey, delivered bread by pony and trap to Ardington.

YOU HAVE TO GET UP EARLY TO SEE RACEHORSE TRAINING ON THE DOWNS; they are back in the stables for breakfast.

THE MILL AT LETCOMBE REGIS is typical of the manorial mills to which all the village corn was taken.

Stanford-in-the-Vale.
S216

Fred. C. Palmer.
Swindon

THE MILL AT STANFORD-IN-THE-VALE is now a private house.

WILLOUGHBY'S MILL in Wantage belonged to the Manor of Priorshold, and probably existed at the time of the Domesday survey. Next to the mill was the Victorian Mill Cottage, where the Willoughbys lived. The mill was working until between the wars.

DANDRIDGE'S MILL at Hanney was a large operation for a village; steam engines and threshing machines were available for hire to local farmers.

The Mill, Wantage.

OPPOSITE THE ENTRANCE TO THE WHARF AT WANTAGE is Clark's Mill; this is the new mill building of c. 1912 which now uses electrically operated machinery. The old stone rollers were kept (and used until recently) in the old mill building on the opposite side of the mill stream. It is a going concern today, selling flour to both local customers and further afield, but the corn ground now is mostly French or Canadian.

Watercress Beds. Letcombe Bassett.

WATERCRESS was grown in most of the spring-line villages, from Ashbury to Blewbury, and shipped daily in season to London. Letcombe's watercress beds are seen best from this bridge over the Brook.

LESLIE TUBB OF LETCOMBE is the last watercress grower of the spring-line villages; he was almost put out of business by the drought of 1976.

MATTHEW REA'S CRESS BEDS at Stowell in Childrey were in use until the 1950s; Pike's Cottage is in the background.

EVERY PARISH HELPED ITS POOR IN SOME WAY through charity administered by its Overseers. These old Parish Rooms in Grove were converted from cottages let to the poor before Grove joined the Wantage Union in 1836. After that the poor had the advantage of Wantage's Workhouse. The cottages were used as a school, and then Parish Rooms, until taken down to build a new Village Hall.

THE FIRE ENGINE used the village pond here in Childrey at the fire on Easter Sunday 1932, which began in the barn, or bakery, of Mr Legge, who was also the postmaster. It destroyed the Post Office and many of the Parish Records kept there.

THESE ALMSHOUSES AT BOURTON are built of the local rag-stone.

THE COVENTRY ALMSHOUSES, Childrey, were opened in 1911 and cost £600. They were for women only, as there were already Fettiplace Almshouses for men and married couples.

A SERIES OF PUBLICITY PHOTOGRAPHS was taken in 1946 for the new Health Service to illustrate improved conditions for the elderly in the new Longworth Hospital. Many had come from Downs Hospital, Wantage, the former Workhouse.

LORD ROBERTS GREETS LADY WANTAGE during army manoeuvres at Watchfield, 1909. The message on the postcard noted that he disliked having his picture taken, but nevertheless agreed to this one.

THIS RED CROSS SEWING PARTY was part of the war effort, 1914–1918, in East Hanney.

THE CANNING UNIT OF EAST HANNEY, with Miss Andrewartha and Mrs Stevens, celebrates VE Day in 1945.

SUPPLY WAGONS wait in Wantage Market Place for loading and transport to the station, 1914–18.

FROM THE NEARBY CAMP AT SHRIVENHAM these army manoeuvres were a common sight.

THIS WATER CISTERN in Faringdon Market Place served the Army during World War II, seen here in a record photograph of 1945.

LEWIS NORTHCOTE practises haymaking with his nanny at East Hendred, c. 1910.

THE CHALK SCHOOL AT UFFINGTON, built in 1617, featured in *Tom Brown's School Days* by Thomas Hughes. Now it is the village museum. Behind it is Jenkins' blacksmith shop, 1916.

BOYS FROM THE SCHOOL AT UFFINGTON work on the allotment gardens, 1910.

THIS GROUP AT THE CHURCH SCHOOL, Watchfield, dates from 1908.

ASHBURY SCHOOLCHILDREN were summoned from class to decorate this country view.

THE NATIONAL SCHOOL on Stanford Road, Faringdon, was built in 1825. The land was given by Mr David Bennett, and it cost one penny a week to attend.

MANY MARKET TOWNS HAD A FEMALE SCHOOL OF INDUSTRY, as here on London Street, Faringdon, founded in 1833.

THIS LITTLE SCHOOLHOUSE replaced the 1526 Elizabethan school house in Childrey. It was built in 1732 by Sir George Fettiplace and his coat of arms can be seen on the gable end. It was in use as a school unit in 1913. Only the end wall with the foundation plaque remains; the school house roof fell into disrepair in spite of Sir John Betjeman's efforts to preserve it.

THE VILLAGE SCHOOL OF LETCOMBE BASSETT is a W. Butterfield design, c. 1870.

AT THE VILLAGE SCHOOL OF LETCOMBE REGIS in 1909, many family names of long standing occur: Palmer, Wilkins, Sims, Goodall, Alder, Froude, Goddings, Addis; some names will be found on the village war memorial.

ST MARY'S SCHOOL, WANTAGE, was founded by the Revd W.J. Butler, for the education of daughters of gentlemen, clergy and professional men. It was staffed by Sisters of the Convent of St Mary, which he also founded. This class is of the 1880s.

THE CLASS OF 1907 of the Church of England primary school in Wantage, brought their toys into this school photograph. Mr H.J. Ireson kept this picture.

MOST VILLAGE SCHOOLS PRACTISED THE MAYPOLE DANCE, as here at Uffington in 1916.

ANOTHER DANCE PRACTISED AT THE MAY DAY CELEBRATIONS is this stick dance, which has obvious links with the Morris Dance. This is at East Hanney School, c. 1910.

THE BOY SCOUT CAMP AT LONGWORTH was the outcome of a friendship between Lt. Col. Granville Walton of the Manor and Lord Baden Powell, founder of the Scout Movement. This meeting was in 1913.

THE GUIDES SOON FOLLOWED THE SCOUTS IN WANTAGE — this is the First King Alfred's Troop photographed by Tom Reveley in 1922. Guide leaders were: centre row, third left, Miss Eileen Adkin (Commandant), fourth left, Miss Olive Griswood, fifth left, Miss Minnie Hughes.

THE COUNTRY PUB WAS OFTEN THE LOCAL SOCIAL CENTRE — here the Old Berkshire Hounds meet at the Lamb and Flag, Longworth. The date on the postcard is 1912.

THIS GROUP OF COURSING ENTHUSIASTS were assembled at Kingston Bagpuize House, home of Mr E.A. Strauss, the Liberal MP in 1906/7. William Jarvis, the boy whose face peers out between the shoulders of two men holding the greyhounds on the front row, remembers the scene well. Many Wantage families are represented: at the top Mr Granger, bank manager; mounted, right, Mr Hanks, the vet, and left, Mr Collard. Next to him, holding the 'slips' is Alf Sansum of the Greyhound pub, Letcombe Regis. John Arbery, the draper, stands by the window's lower right corner, near the elderly Mr Nicholls, the stationer. The lady in the centre, with a scarf tied around her hat, is the wife of the photographer, Tom Reveley; behind her and to the right is Mr Jarvis' mother and Arthur Belcher.

THIS TURN-OF-THE-CENTURY POLITICAL MEETING on Uffington Common attracted people from nearby villages also.

'LIVING BRIDGE' was performed at the Faringdon Flower Show in July 1906.

THE FIFE AND DRUM BAND was founded and led by bandmaster A.V. Gibbs, standing, second from right. They met at the King Alfred's Head pub, but there was no drinking, smoking or swearing.

THE LONGWORTH CLUB met at the Lamb and Flag, and were photographed by Henry Taunt.

LOCALS SIT OUTSIDE THE HARE AT WEST HENDRED, with Mr and Mrs Frank Quartermain. Left to right: Mrs Quartermain, W. Saunders, Frank Quartermain, (seated); Goddard, –?–, –?–, Roberts (standing), –?–, G. Stater (standing), E. Welsh (seated), Shepherd, J. Castle (standing), T. Castle (seated), Mulford (standing), K. Roberts (seated), –?–, B. Harries, c. 1910.

FRED MULFORD poses outside the Hare, now tile-hung, in the 1930s.

THE ABINGDON TRADITIONAL MORRIS DANCERS perform at Faringdon in 1939. The Mayor of Ock Street was Henry Hemmings, the musician was Harry Thomas and the Hornbearer was Jack Hyde.

MEMBERS OF THE WANTAGE AND DISTRICT FIELD CLUB inspect the building site on Littleworth Hill – finds of Roman pottery and coins over the years indicated Roman settlement there, and excavations took place over the next year 1973/74. Left to right: Mrs Jean Naish, Mrs Jean Banford, Miss Kathleen Philip, Dr Thomas Ridsdill-Smith.

CRICKET was introduced at King Alfred's School, Wantage, in the 1870s.

W. A. NOBLE   F. HANKINS   G. SHOREY   A. JOHNSON   A. BUNCE
(Secretary)   (Linesman)
              M. HISKINS   A. BUNCE   W. PIERPOINT

WANTAGE TOWN FOOTBALL CLUB in 1909. Back, left to right: W.A. Noble, Secretary; F. Hankins, G. Shorey, A. Johnson, A. Burcel (linesman). Front, left to right: M. Hiskins, A. Bunce, W. Pierpoint.

THE CYCLING CLUB met at the Bear and had Lord Wantage as its President for many years.

AT WANTAGE, celebrations for the Coronation in 1911 took place at Stirlings Field, watched by this crowd of lovely hats.

THE COURTYARD OF STILES ALMSHOUSES, Wantage, is decorated for the coronation of King George V and Queen Mary, 1911.

SCENES FROM THE WANTAGE CARNIVAL held to celebrate peace in 1919. Nobly Chapman is the clown seated on the right (opposite, top). The football says 'Peace 1919'.

BILL DENNIS IN THE TIE AND LESLIE HUGHES IN THE CAP stand behind the chef at the Coronation Ox Roast in 1937, Wantage Market Place.

THIS WEDDING PARTY took place near Kingston Lisle in 1900, a photograph kept by Mr Taylor, whose uncles and mother are the children in the front row.

THIS SOMBRE VICTORIAN FAMILY LIVED AT FRAMLANDS, on the edge of Wantage in the 1880s. The father is Judge Makonochie.

HARPER, THE WIERKEEPER OF RADCOT, is seen in an early Henry Taunt photograph of the 1870s.

MISS LAVINIA SMITH of Downside, East Hendred, made a private museum of local agricultural equipment and bygones. At her death, in the 1950s, the collection went to the Museum of English Rural Life at Reading.

THE PHOTOGRAPHER TOM REVELEY OF WANTAGE is usually remembered for his country scenes and family portraits, but this is a wonderful, informal portrait study.

THE FIRST MRS SILVER of the Manor, Letcombe Regis, was known to drive into Wantage with her pet lion in the back seat of her open car.

THE ROUND HOUSE AT HINTON WALDRIST is one of the most well-known turnpike toll houses on the Oxford–Swindon road. A stone quarry lay behind it.

A BERKSHIRE WAGON, drawn by shire horses with their harness brasses gleaming, carries corn at Buckland.

THE FERRY ACROSS THE RIVER THAMES AT DUXFORD, Hinton Waldrist, must have been an uncomfortable experience from 1827–1920.

UFFINGTON WAS A BUSY PLACE, with a rail station, canal wharf, several smiths and wheelwrights, a malthouse and brickworks. The bridge over the canal, hoist and wharf lie behind the house, seen here in 1916.

BRIDGE COTTAGE, also on the Canal, lay at Knighton Turn, Uffington, 1916. The Wilts and Berks Canal opened in 1810 and linked the Vale of the White Horse from the Thames at Abingdon to Semington in Wiltshire, near Swindon.

THE HISKINS FAMILY ran the Wharf at Wantage – the house where they lived is in the background – built of stone brought by the canal 1810–20. The Wharfinger's house and the stable can still be seen near the filled-in Wharf basin off Mill Street.

THE WHARF at the town end of the Wantage Arm of the Wilts and Berks Canal became grown over soon after traffic ceased around 1900. The terrace opposite, Wharf Terrace, once a lively group of houses and a pub, gradually became derelict and was taken down in the early 70s.

THE WANTAGE ARM linked the Wharf with the main Wilts and Berks Canal two miles away, at Grove.

PINMARSH BRIDGE took the road over the Canal between Lockinge and Ardington.

GROVE TOP LOCK, with its lock-keeper's cottage, was one of a flight of seven through the village, which also had its own wharf. This was around 1900, when the life of the Canal was nearly over.

FROM 1864 FARINGDON HAD A BRANCH LINE TO UFFINGTON STATION on the main Great Western Railway line which opened in 1840. This photograph dates from 1919.

WANTAGE ROAD STATION was still equipped with old broad gauge track up until 1919.

A DONKEY AND TRAP takes the ladies to Wantage from the Manor at Letcombe.

HERE IS AN AFFECTIONATE LOOK AT THE WANTAGE TRAMWAY, one of several circulating at the time. The donkey laughing away is probably Arthur Hitchcock's 'moke' who reputedly won a race with the tram.

THE WANTAGE TRAMWAY opened in 1875; the office on Mill Street was given a new red brick facing in 1904. The line linked Wantage with Wantage Road Station on the Great Western Railway 2½ miles to the north. Apart from locals travelling on the GWR the biggest customers were for the good service: Clark's Mill, Weedons Coal, Wantage Engineering Company.

THE TOWN TERMINUS and passenger platform were behind the Mill Street offices; now the shed is bricked up for storage and garages.

THE GOODS YARD WAS NEXT TO THE WHARF; the lifting crane you can see was purchased from the Canal Company, after the canal closed.

DRIVER WEAVING AND TRAMWAY STAFF pose with Engine No. 7, the Manning Wardle Saddle Tank.

AT GROVE BRIDGE there was a passing loop, but the line crossed the turnpike road ungated. The whistle warned motor traffic of its approach, but was hardly necessary with the small number of cars on the country road. The most frequent accidents were derailments due to the condition of the track.

THE LAST ENGINE IN SERVICE WAS SHANNON, known locally as Jane, seen here on a siding at Wantage Road Station in 1948, after closure of the Tramway Company.

WITH *JANE,* ENGINE NO. 5, are Mr Widridge, signalman, and Mr Powell (with the hat) the station master, after restoration of the engine at the Swindon works. *Jane* is now at the Great Western Railway Museum at Didcot, where she can occasionally be seen in steam.

THE FIRST MOTOR IN WANTAGE was owned by Mr L. Pates; he also provided traction for the steam fire engine. Here he is driving with Mr F. Brooks in 1906.

THE WI OF EAST HANNEY take a charabanc outing in the mid 1920s. The omnibus made such outings, usually to seaside towns, accessible to many more people – but the day might begin at 6 a.m. as it took four hours to reach Southampton.

THE CHOIR PARTY TO BOURNMOUTH FROM EAST HANNEY, July 1923: Mr Noon, vicar; Mr Clinch, sexton; Mr Edwards, Headmaster. On the charabanc: C. Higgs, F. Bunce, G. Tombs, R. Breakspear, J. Bunce, E.H.W. & C. Cox, F. Daubney, V. Lamble, G. Burnett, G. Belcher, E. Cowie, F. Monk, J. Adams, D. Barrett, C. Barrow, J. Broughton, L. Clinch, W. Spinloe.

THE OMNIBUS CALLS IN AT THE ROSE AND CROWN, ASHBURY. This service made shopping in the market towns easier for country people; it opened up town and city jobs and marked the beginning of real suburban life.

WHO WOULD HAVE THOUGHT THAT THE COMING OF THE MOTOR CAR WOULD LEAD TO THIS in the 50 years that separate these two photographs? A demonstration for a bypass for Faringdon holds up a lorry in the Market Place, December 1972.

ACKNOWLEDGEMENTS

Abingdon Museum • Mrs Akers • Mrs O. Ashthorpe • Miss S. Baker
Mrs J. Banford • Berkshire Archaeological Society • Mr A. W. Bourne
Mr D. Bradbrook • Miss C. Bradford • Mrs A. C. Castle • Mrs P. Childerley
Mrs J. Clayton • Mr J. Collier • Mrs M. Crook • Mr W. Dennis • Mr N. Eady
Mrs Eltham • Mr M. E. Eyre • Mr R. Fairfull • Mrs C. B. Fewins
Mr W. Fuller • Mr A. H. Gregory • Mr W. Hiskins • Mr T. Hook
Mr L. Hughes • Mrs S. Hughes • Mr H. J. Ireson • Mr R. James
Mr W. Jarvis • Mrs Lewis-Price • Mr J. Loftin • Mrs J. Loudon
Miss E. Lovegrove • Mr M. Murfett • National Monuments Record
Oxfordshire County Libraries • Oxford Mail and Times
Oxfordshire Museums Service • Oxford Publishing Company • Mrs L. Pates
Penny's Menswear • Miss K. Philip • Miss M. Powell • Reading Museum
Mrs W. Silver • Mr F. B. Simkins • Mrs J. Smith • Dr R. Squires
Mr W. Stanley • Swindon Museum • Mr Taylor • Mrs Theobold
Vale and Downland Museum Centre, Wantage

Wherever possible the original donor or lender of a photograph has been acknowledged. Those from the various institutions and museums, after all, represent many individual donations. Another invaluable contribution has been the help in identifying and dating the photographs, and providing background information, often from personal memory, which has been so freely given by colleagues, owners and lenders. I should particularly like to thank Daphne Jones for her help in assembling the material and Sue Etchells for typing it.

Nancy Hood
October 1987